1

Disclaimer and Copyright

It is with my utmost sincerity that I write a plethora of suggestions which may improve your life. The metaphor clearly states that YOU are in charge. I wish a life full of health, happiness and success for you. If, for whatever reason, you fail to attain that goal or dream, please understand that there can be no legal ramifications of your expectations or your desired outcome specifically due to my suggestions in my book.

This book can be used as a textbook and portions can be copied for educational lessons. Please ask for permission for any other circumstances. Copying the entire book and using all its contents is strictly prohibited.

Tom Kidd
tomdebki@triwest.net
715-456-4856

ISBN 9781099353611

Contact Information
Tom Kidd
Balanced Wellness Services
www.kidd4kids.org
www.intentionallivinguniversity.com
tomdebki@triwest.net
1-715-456-4856

Testimonials

"Tom has provided a clear, easy to follow formula that is applicable and important to everyone regardless of background or profession. As each of us nears the end of our days and reflect on how much we lived our life, I can think of nothing more important than being satisfied with the experience. Some lucky few get there entirely by chance, but why leave such momentous decisions to luck? Tom has converted many years of thought and experience into an easy to read guide that will lead you through self-examination and help you craft a custom plan for yourself. I already am thinking about the rest of my life and I do have a plan as a result of this book. I believe there is great value in writing it out as well.

Enjoy the ride!"

Matthew Barre CDR (ret) USCG M.P.A. Commercial Pilot

"WHAT?... I'M Flying the Plane?" was one of the most practical, comprehensive and effective personal empowerment books I've read to date. The checklists and action plans at the end of each chapter make the change process very attainable and set you up for massive success. If you're looking for a holistic perspective on how to create regenerative heart-felt change, this is your book. It motivated me to re-write my "life's mission statement."

Matt D'Amour-Owner of Inside Out Wellness- Certified Life Coach

"I thoroughly enjoyed this book. It offers many opportunities for personal reflection, analysis and direction of one's life."

John Modjeski- B.S. M.S. Ed Retired Educator/Administrator

Contents

—

4

—

5

Acknowledgements

Special thanks to Kathie Trzecinski, a dear friend and former colleague of mine for facilitating the editing of the book. Special thanks as well to Rachael Bejin for her expertise in the publishing of this book.

Manuscript proofreaders:

Matt Barre
Rozanna Bejin
Matt D'Amour
Dr. Dick Detert
Madison Kidd
John and Jane Modjeski
Jim Reppe
Elaine Rizzuto
Dan Slowey
David Winograd

Dedication

This book is dedicated to my wife's 104-year-old grandmother who passed away on Friday, April 12, 2019. I believe she is still living in many of us, especially me as I finish writing this book. Terese Powers, who we lovingly called Gigi, will always be an absolute, profound living legend. She had aged with happiness, grace and dignity and now has landed at her destination. She has inspired me to share some of my thoughts, actions and beliefs. I asked her for her secret ingredients to longevity. She typed these out for me. Each one on a of 3 x 5 notecard from her Smith-Corona ribbon electric typewriter:

- Be thankful
- Be kind to everyone you meet
- Have faith

- Move
- Eat well
- Love
- Trust
- Laugh often
- Take time for self and others
- Volunteer

It is with utmost respect and honor that I dedicate this book to her; a book that could alter the lives of millions. Gigi will always be a living example of how you can PLAN your life and live it with intention, balance, love and passion.

Gigi, may you continue to watch over all of us and inspire all who read this book with the possibility of living a new journey. Sincere thanks for all your love, words of wisdom and direction in my life.

God bless you, Gigi!

Author's Note

In all my years of presenting to educators, employees, students, parents and attendees from various organizations, I have made it my focus to provide them not only with new and relevant information about specific topics, but the necessary skills to complement them. I believe, it is only then, that sustainable behaviors can change and action can occur. It is with these skills and knowledge to which I intentionally blend an emotional tie, that cements the learning experience.

As I've continued to speak at various venues, many have asked, "Do you have more of what you spoke on in a book?" I then decided to assimilate and condense a significant share of my presentations into one book with additional added information to include stories and life skills.

In this book, you will come to understand that I truly believe in altering lives in a very positive way. I am relentless about intentionally promoting lives that include more passion, balance and purpose.

I am extremely excited you have chosen this book to read. It may drastically change or alter your life *forever!* It is my sincere desire to cordially invite you to integrate the knowledge and skills you are about to read, while taking a journey into your life which you may never have taken before.

Enjoy every moment of your journey designing, planning and creating a vision for the remainder of your life!

Foreword

*There is only one corner of the universe
you can be certain of changing, and that is
yourself*

A. Huxley

As a health education specialist, I have been intrigued for years in what creates success when trying to assist others as they endeavor to bring about positive health changes in their lives. There are many health behavior change models that professionals use to facilitate change. Many of these models are excellent approaches for successful change. In this book, you will encounter a couple of these models. However, these models are only part of what creates successful change.

I would like to share the insights of four very successful individuals. You won't see their names in this book, but you will recognize their ideas imbedded within the chapters Tom provides. These ideas come from three very successful businessmen and one sports figure. These insights are not only intended for the enterprises they represent but for anyone desiring to make positive changes in their life. Here is what they have to say. Be sure to look for them as you move through the chapters.

Warren Buffet: *Find your passion; Model the success of others* by engaging them in conversation, asking questions and using their experiences when making changes.

Steve Jobs: *Design for Yourself* by engaging in activities that will work best for you. Also, follow your *values*. These are not just any values, but core values that touch the soul so you can change health for the better personally, at work and at home.

Bill Gates: *Create the future you want, enjoy what your do every day and ask for advice.* Above all, do not procrastinate. Get started and keep working on your plan with a sense of humor.

Michael Jordan: *Have high expectations, be positive, have a vision and practice.* You may not be playing basketball but think about why they call it "mindfulness practice, relaxation practice, meditation practice, yoga practice," and the like. Whether you are playing a sport or trying to improve a healthy behavior, the goal is to eliminate thinking about it so that the behavior becomes automatic.

While reading this book, I realized how masterfully Tom used the flight metaphor. A metaphor where he uses his personal experiences as an educator, contemporary behavior-change strategies and the ideas from the above four individuals to weave a personal flight action plan to improve your life. The thirteen chapters become the building blocks for successful life changes. The personal stories, information, planning and practice, along with supplemental resources will keep you engaged throughout the entire process. Or as Tom might say, *the entire flight.* There is no hurry, preaching or judgments. So, as you proceed along this journey, be sure to stop, turn around, reflect and enjoy the view. And remember:

Your wings already exist
All you have to do is fly
Author Unknown

Dr. Richard Detert
Professor Emeritus, author, researcher,
educator, life-long learner

Introduction

Are you ready for take-off?

Congratulations! You have picked up this book to either read or are reading the introduction because you are simply inquisitive about its contents! Whatever your intention, this book will take you on an extremely exciting journey. **It is a book about purposely planning the remaining time you have to live *YOUR LIFE!*** In reality, that could be days, weeks, months or hopefully many years. It really doesn't matter if you are young or older. It doesn't matter if you are working or retired. If you simply believe in fate directing the rest of your life, then I believe you will continue to wake up daily and "allow things to just happen." Some things may be good, some may be bad, some may be intended, some not. Time may be flying away from you too rapidly to intentionally live with more passion and purpose. However, it is my intention, this book will instill much hope and encouragement for you.

Each chapter has a different topic, a sub heading to draw your interest, and at the end of each chapter you will see a Safe Flight Checklist which includes main ideas from the chapter. Also, you will find your Flight Action Plan which are suggestions for you to take immediate action on regarding the topic. And last but not least, you'll be given an invitation to visit a Companion Website for more related articles and suggested books or video clips on that specific topic.

Imagine this metaphor for a moment. YOU are *piloting* an airplane just as you may be the *pilot* of your life. You are in control of its ride, its destination and its landing. Wouldn't you agree that time flies? Begin to realize you are the pilot of your life and all its remaining time.

If you have the desire to refocus and rejuvenate your life with passion, purpose and a plan, then this book will allow for an unbelievable transformation of your life that will allow you to live more happily, with more satisfaction and with few regrets. This book will help you on a personal journey to "get off the fast-paced roller-coaster" of present-day life and just slow down enough to contemplate and plan out the rest of your life. This purposeful plan written with passion will be complete with a chosen daily attitude, achievable goals, daily reminders and a clear vision for the rest of your life. A vision for HOW you want SPEND your time and LIVE your life!

I welcome you to an opportunity that may alter the way you live. I encourage you to read this book, and in doing so, begin to live differently. To live with more passion, direction and purpose. This is all possible because of a written plan carefully designed by YOU. It will be used as a daily reminder on how YOU want to live each and every day for the rest of your life.

This book is primarily written about YOU being in control. By no means does this relate to it being secular. As you will learn more about the control you have and the vision for yourself, many people include their higher power such as their faith, their God or their spirit, etc. as their *Control Tower Communicator* or as their *co-pilot*. I encourage you to feel free to assimilate your core values, beliefs and spirit into your eventual vision, plan and mission.

As a pilot prepares their VFR or Visual Flight Rules, so will you be encouraged to look at a myriad of checklists to determine if you are ready to fly. A pilot sees the horizon and orients the aircraft by reference to the earth as he/she observes it. When entering the clouds, a pilot has to revert to the IFR or the Instrument Flight Rules. Just like in our lives, we need a different set of rules or a plan "when things get cloudy." In most aircrafts today, there is an ADI or an Altitude Direction Indicator. In life, sometimes you'll need a ADI or an Attitude Detection Indicator. I'll talk more about your attitude in chapter five.

I encourage you to walk the boarding ramp and proudly walk through the airplane door to begin creating a refocused and rejuvenated life. I challenge you to open the cockpit door and climb into the pilot seat as you read this book and begin your journey. Be the architect while thoroughly enjoying the process of identifying, developing, writing and then living your life's *flight plan.*

WELCOME ABOARD!

Chapter 1

Welcome to the Journey
"You are the pilot for the rest of your life's flight"

Welcome to the rest of your life! Let's begin this exciting new journey by choosing your life's direction with an open mind, an open heart, and an attitude full of anticipation and hope. Together, let's begin planning for the rest of your life; yes, at your age! Age doesn't matter here. What does matter are the plans you have for the years ahead. As you read this book, my expectation for you is to plan and write your journey, while enjoying the process and beginning to live intentionally.

Remember, you are the pilot of your life. Your life depends solely on you, not someone who may be your co-pilot. As you read, I ask that you reflect on your innermost emotions, your core values, beliefs, and the lifestyle you want to live. Stop every few paragraphs, pages or chapters to ask yourself, "How do I feel about this? What am I thinking? How does this relate to me?" Then identify those thoughts and feelings by writing down some ideas regarding your spirit, core passion and what motivates you.

Let's start with the thought process of treating your body like a car. Let's say you were told at age 16, when you secured your driver's license, you would be GIVEN a car. However, this would be the only car you would have for the rest of your life. It must last a lifetime. Would you take care of that car differently under that condition? Would you make sure you did the regular maintenance?

- Would you pour floor cleaner into your gas tank? NO, yet many people abuse alcohol or drugs.
- Would you empty your vacuum cleaner contents in the carburetor? NO, yet many people smoke cigarettes or marijuana.
- Would you give it the correct amount of oil to keep the pistons lubricated? YES, then drink plenty of water and exercise daily.
- Would you give it quality fuel? YES, then eat the proper foods in proper proportion.

Your body is that vehicle. You have been given one body and one mind and THEY have to last you a lifetime! How are you taking care of your car? If you wish to plan for your future life, you have to appreciate what you have right now. This metaphor should help put your health and gifts you have been given into perspective.

I would like to provide a rare and special opportunity for you to STOP, REFLECT and DEVELOP a PLAN for what you would like to do with priceless years you have left to live - *your flight* and *your landing.* This will allow you to look back after landing and say, "It was a great flight! I have no regrets!" In order for this to happen, you have to realistically assess where you are right now and where it is you want to go.

Let us use yet, another metaphor. Let's compare your life to a 78-foot rope. The average life expectancy is about 78 years; each foot represents one year of life. From ages birth to 6, the first six feet, are the infancy and early childhood years. During this time, primarily

---

all of our life's survival decisions are made for us. From ages 6-12, the next six feet, are the elementary school ages when decisions are made by us, our parents, our teachers and others close to us in our environment. In most instances, we are not thinking about any decisions that may affect the future of our life.

From ages 13-17, we all know what happens. Friends and hormones direct our thinking. This is a critical time of decision making on our rope due to influences by our peers, culture and social media. Many times, youth at this age make decisions without realizing the long-term impact. This is when decisions made could influence the rest of our lives. However, parents and mentors still have a significant influence on decisions made by this age group.

From ages 18-24, another six feet, brings independent living. Usually a person will move out of the family home and will make decisions on their own. However, research has shown the pre-frontal cortex of the brain, the frontal lobe of our brain, which allows for moral reasoning and the ability to foresee consequences does not fully develop until the age of 21! This research is exactly why the legal drinking age was raised from 18 to 21 across the United States. Between the ages of 18 and 24, many well-mannered and well-intentioned young men and women make life-altering decisions that affect their futures. Some do well, some simply "get through" and some unfortunately falter.

From ages 24-30, another six years, is where one usually begins to settle down, to become more responsible and to better make decisions. The pre-frontal cortex has been fully developed and allows one to think with the entire brain. One may get more serious about a job or a career. Yet, even at this stage, one may still neglect to foresee how decisions and choices will affect the rest of their life. And so here we are, most of us reading this book at the age of 30 and older trying to make a living but not making a life.

Now is the time for you to plan your life's flight. Your plan will address the eight dimensions of wellness: social, physical, emotional, career, intellectual, environmental, spiritual, and financial. At the same time, this plan will include a balance in your personal, professional and family life. Even though you may be in midflight, you still can adjust your flight's course to ensure a smooth and enjoyable *flight*.

The first step to planning is to identify your reason, your purpose and the WHY you fly your plane. Why do you get up every day? What for? For whom? You have a choice: to plan or not to plan. If you choose not to plan, you basically are allowing fate to take you on your plane ride. This choice often leads to complacency with regrets. If you choose to plan, you will be heading toward living the life you have always wanted.

I would like to share a personal story that has allowed me to think, feel and begin to live differently all by my choice. I made this choice with passion and have no regrets.

About 20 years ago, I was invited to off-road mountain biking event with friends. I wasn't totally keen on the idea but agreed. I purchased an $800 bike and started to train on-road. I had trained for 4-5 weeks when one of the crew members asked me if I'd like to ride in an upcoming off-road race. The race distance was 15 or 40 miles. I hesitantly agreed to the 15-mile race.

As we arrived at the race site, I looked around. I could see I was inadequately prepared. I felt that sick, nervous feeling in the pit of my stomach that we all usually get when we are about to embark on something new and challenging. I had basketball shorts; they had Under Armor bicycle pants. I had an old cut-off t-shirt; they had fitted biking shirts. They had the sleek helmets; I had one from the early 70's. They had riding shoes that locked into the pedals of the bike; I had tennis shoes used for running. I felt humbled. They were all preoccupied spinning their tires, checking their air pressures and gear-chain operation. I walked around aimlessly. One of my friends noticed my discomfort and some of my nervousness and suggested I go register. I got my race number, put it on my t-shirt and ate the granola bar that came in the registration bag. My confidence grew a bit, although it was very minimal.

Soon officials began sending riders off in groups according to their experience. Naturally, the more experienced and competitive bikers were called first. One of my friends and I were standing at the top of the hill watching the groups begin. I wishfully asked him, "Would you start last with me and ride the first mile with me? Just get me going; after the first mile, feel free to go at your own pace." He thankfully agreed. Just then a young man rode up next to me on his bike and asked me, "Is this your first race?" I chuckled, "Is it that obvious?" He asked if I was going to ride the 15-mile or the 40-mile race. I told him I was *attempting* the 15-mile. He shared with me that this would be his 8th time riding the 40-mile that summer. As he rode away, he wished my friend and me good luck. And then I noticed it. He had only one leg! Yes, a prosthetic device attached to his right leg that was locked into his shoe which locked into the bike pedal. It was at that moment I told my friend, who agreed to ride the first mile with me, that I wanted to be the very last person to start the race. I also decided to turn off my odometer (gauge for miles) and to turn off my speedometer (rate of miles per hour). I, by intention, decided that I was going to ride *my race* and enjoy it.

And so, I began, after all the others had started ahead of me. My pace was even. I was alone. I felt free and in charge! I really didn't care who won the race. I didn't care how fast I was going, how many miles I had gone, and I didn't care about my finish time. My thinking was, "I'm going to enjoy this ride!" After a short time of leisurely riding, I got off my bike and laid on my back among the tall blades of grass. Lying there in a comfortable and rested position, I slowly looked up to the sky above. The sky was an absolutely gorgeous blue. The pine trees filled the air with their sweet aroma. I took a thick piece of grass and placed it between my thumbs and tried to make that whistling sound as I'm sure many of us have tried at one time when we were kids. I felt joy. I felt peace. I felt control.

I continued to bike to the first water station. Everyone tried to hand me water and encouraged me to get back on course as quickly as possible. I intentionally got off my bike and began to shake hands while introducing myself to all the volunteers. I was in no particular hurry. I intentionally fought the desire to compete. I chatted with the volunteers and even shared a joke or two. And, before I took off riding again, I splattered some water on the front of my t-shirt humorously wanting to give the impression to others that I had been sweating, working hard and competing.

There was a dichotomy – the race I was in and the race in my life. After a few more miles, I chose to stop once again near a babbling brook, rested and simply listened to the stillness. I rode for a lengthier amount of time and then stopped again in a dandelion field. I laid down and looked slowly around me at the most beautiful dandelions I had ever seen, the bluest sky and the breath-taking sight of hundreds of green forest trees.

Biking, stopping by intention, and just enjoying my ride was an absolute mind-altering and rejuvenating experience. For the first time, I realized I could live my life much like the way I approached this race. I traveled a few more miles and I saw something I didn't actually want to see. Yes, it was the finish line. A line most racers yearn to see as quickly as possible. Not for me; the finish line signaled to me that it was all going to end too soon. Before I entered the chute, I could see and hear finished bikers cheering for me. I quickly splattered more water on my shirt. I again wanted to look like I had really worked up a sweat and raced. Riding through that chute, being cheered on by all who finished before me, was a definite high. They were celebrating "my finish." This gives a whole new meaning of "celebration of life," doesn't it?

I had finished that race because I PLANNED my ride as well as PLANNED for my finish. My plan to shut off my speedometer (slow down), shut off my odometer (not care how far I went) and get off the bike and LIVE were remarkable ones. I was on an intentional mission with a purpose specifically designed by me.

So, I would like to challenge you to become a priority in your life WITH a plan. This plan certainly may include a spouse, a friend, a significant other, your God, etc. as a co-pilot. Sometimes it is easier to *fly a plane* with two people striving towards a safe flight. Know that when your life is *on course* with its purpose and direction, you are most powerful, effective and successful. Allow me to help you begin the process of writing or drawing up your architectural design, your blueprint, your foundation, your plan for the remaining years of your life. Once this is accomplished, you will have a reminder, guide and plan to read daily, live by, and truly live the rest of your rope as you enjoy the rest of *your flight.* Let's get after it right now and begin to live with more intention, more purpose, more passion by design! Feel the power of being the pilot of your life.

SAFE FLIGHT CHECKLIST:

- YOU are the pilot of the rest of your life.
- Treat your mind and body like a once in a lifetime car.
- Consider how you want to live the rest of your *rope.*
- Personally, design and plan for the remaining years of your life.

YOUR FLIGHT ACTION PLAN:

1. Look up the definition of the word "journey." Think about the definition and write down some general thoughts on how you would like your life's journey to play out.

2. Brainstorm and write down bits of your vision or plan of where you'd like to be in 5-30 years in regard to your personal self, work, career, family, etc. Enjoy the process.

3. Within the next three days, discuss your rope analogy with someone. Share how you will design your plan so that you will have no regrets during your flight and its final landing destination.

   - Go to the companion website at **www.intentionallivinguniversity.com** for more articles, suggested books, video clips, etc.

Chapter 2

Choosing Your Life's Direction
"Looking for Another Flight Pattern?"

Let's get ready for *take-off*. There are mandatory checks a pilot must make before departure. Like pilots, we also need to prepare for the *flight* we are about to embark. Choosing your life's direction may sound fairly simple. Nonetheless, before departing, your vision should take some deep thought, careful consideration and intentional planning.

Are you living your life to the fullest? Are you happy, satisfied and content with what you are doing and who you are? Have you planned to live the remaining portion of your life so that there are few if any regrets? If you want any input on your future lifestyle, choosing your direction at this point in your life is crucial. If you are looking for another *flight pattern* or *landing strip*, a different way of living, as you *pilot* your life, now is the time to think and plan. Don't waste any more time possibly heading down the runway in the wrong direction.

The following quote ought to reassure you that it is never too late to choose a different direction. "A PERSON IS NOT OLD UNTIL REGRETS TAKE THE PLACE OF PLANS AND DREAMS."

Hopefully, when you are 70, 80, 90, maybe even 100 years old and sitting in your rocking chair, you will be able to look back on your life and know that you have had minimal regrets. After all, we are human and when we look back at our lives, we'll all still probably regret a few things because of our human nature. Imagine if you observed a flashing alarm on your plane's instrument panel stating WARNING: flying without instruments, flying too fast, watch out for what is ahead, etc. That would be alarming. Intentionally designing how you want to live for the rest of your life does not just happen by fate. It happens by deliberate thinking, planning and setting your desired goals. And that reality comes to life when you begin to take specific actions and live according to the plan specifically designed by you.

As you choose your life's direction, you need to consider the aging process. We are aging every second, every minute, every hour, every day and every year. The fear of getting old seems to frighten and threaten us. Quite often, it is fear that prevents us from planning our future. Yet, fear should motivate us to plan before *we land our plane.*

Reflect on the following quotes regarding aging:
- Growing OLD is inevitable, growing UP is optional.
- Age is mind over matter. If you don't mind, it doesn't matter.
- You can't help growing older, but you don't have to get old.

Do you realize the only time we want to get older is when we were kids? If you are less than ten years old, you think in fractions. When asked, "How old are you?" Kids usually respond with, "I'm four and a half." Adults don't say we are forty and a half. Teens respond by stating, "I'm gonna be 16." They could be 13; but hey, they are eventually gonna be 16. And then, the greatest day of your life arrives when you *become* 21. Even saying "twenty-one" sounds like a ceremony. But then you *turn* 30. Oooohhh, what happened? Thirty makes one sound like spoiled milk. They *turned* 30. What's wrong? What has changed? Before you know it, you are *pushing* 40! Whoa! Pushing 40? Let's put on the brakes! It's all slipping away quickly. In a blink of an eye, you *reach* 50. Oh, but wait, you *make it* to 60. You have now built up so much speed that you *hit* 70. Once you are in your 80's, every day becomes a cycle: each day you *become* another day older: you *hit* lunch, you *turn* 4:30 and you *reach* bedtime.

It doesn't end here. When you are in your 90's, you begin to count backwards, "I was *just* 92." Then the strangest thing happens. If you make it to 100, you become like a little kid again. "I'm 100 and a half." I honestly hope everyone reading this book will live to at least a healthy 100 and a half! Don't let aging prevent you from planning your life.

Are you spending enough time on your priorities? The first step to changing your life's direction is to identify your life's priorities: the things you live and get up for every day. Once those have been identified, ask yourself if your life is balanced personally, professionally and with family. This balance will be an essential part of your plan.

Consider the following thoughts when thinking about your life and your priorities:

- Yesterday is history...tomorrow is a mystery...and today is a gift...that's why they call it...the *present.*
- Your daily gratitude and appreciation will help you with your future life's direction.
- Vince Lombardi, legendary coach of the Green Bay Packers once said, "If you're not fired up with enthusiasm, you'll be fired with enthusiasm."
- It is never too late to choose the direction for the remaining portion of your life.

Who said, "The saddest person is a person that has sight but no vision?" If you said Helen Keller, you are correct. Having no vision for the direction of your life is extremely sad. But you are about to change that by directing or re-directing your *flight pattern*, your life's course.

Having written goals that are realistic, attainable and visible is critical to helping you choose your life's direction. Written goals have a way of transforming wishes into wants, cant's into cans, dreams into plans and plans into reality. DON'T JUST THINK IT, INK IT.

In one of the upcoming chapters, I will provide you the opportunity to create your very own bucket list: those life achievements you want to accomplish before you kick the bucket. Maybe even a spousal bucket list or a family bucket list may be in order. Writing yours and posting them may just re-direct your life.

Another important aspect of choosing a new direction is caring for yourself. You need to make YOURSELF are a priority so that you will be healthy and well enough to live the life you are directing. You wouldn't want the pilot of the plane you are on to be at risk for a heart attack or stroke, would you? Putting your health first is crucial while developing your life's plan. Sadly, in many cases, waiting until retirement to do the many things you would like to do may be too late. I have attended all too many funerals for my colleagues who died way too soon because they had not realized the importance of taking care of themselves. A friend of mine had it right. He believed he needed to spend more time intentionally working on staying healthy, so that when he reached his years of retirement, he could reap the benefits of being healthy. His plan was to be healthy enough to thoroughly enjoy the many activities he chose to live for in his flight plan!

So, how do we really choose our life's direction and then plan it wisely? I would like to share a story from an unknown author about a builder.

An elderly carpenter was ready to retire. He told his employer-contractor of his plan to leave the home-building business and live a more leisurely life with his wife while enjoying his sons, daughters and grandchildren more often. He felt he would miss the paycheck but knew they could get by financially. The contractor was sorry to see his good builder leave and asked if he would be willing to build just one more home as a personal favor for the company. The builder agreed. But in time, it was easy to see that his heart was not in his work. He resorted to shoddy workmanship and more often used inferior materials. It was an unfortunate way to end his productive career and reputation for quality workmanship. When the builder finished his work and the contractor came to inspect the house, the contractor handed him the keys to the home. "This is your home," he said. "It's my gift to you." What a shock! What a shame! IF the builder had only known he was building his own home, he would have done it all so differently. Now he was forced to live in a poorly built house. A house that was built without a plan; it had no purpose or passion.

It is the same with us. We build our lives in distracted ways without direction or without a plan. We react rather than act. We are willing to put up with less than our best efforts to *build* our home. At several important points in our lives, we may neglect to check out the *blueprints,* our plan to live the life we want or the *home* in which we want to live. Think of yourself as a builder for a moment. Think about the home, the life you are building. Every day you hammer a nail, place a board or erect a wall. Build wisely. It is the only life you will ever build. The plaque on your new home should read, "Life is a do-it-yourself" project. Your life should always be under construction. It is the result of a detailed plan with choices, attitudes and a purpose. Your life tomorrow, *your new home*, will be the direct result of the choices and plans you make today.

If you don't decide to *fly* your plane or plan for the rest of your life, you will always be at the whim of everyone else's travel plans. Understand that this is your plane and your trip. With your renewed passion and energy, you can rally your passengers: your spouse, your family, your colleagues and your friends. Have them enjoy your flight as well. Go ahead, grab that dual joystick steering mechanism in front of you as you comfortably sit in the cockpit and begin changing your flight direction. Know that you'll stay on your flight pattern towards the landing destination you desire. When you feel like you are in charge of the plane, *your life*, you will reclaim a sense of power. Aspects of your life will begin to change: your relationships, your job, your satisfaction and happiness. So, grow older but don't grow up; live your life to the fullest and enjoy the ride by choosing your own direction.

The rest of this book will aid you in planning the remaining portion of your *flight* so you can *land well* and appreciate the happy, healthy and successful trip you have taken with your plan.

SAFE FLIGHT CHECKLIST:

- Think of your aging process differently.
- Focus and spend time on your priorities.
- Care for YOU by making yourself a priority.
- Intentionally design how you want to live the rest of your life.

YOUR FLIGHT ACTION PLAN:

1. Identify and make a list of negative behaviors that are preventing you from living the life you might prefer.

2. Talk to your spouse, family member, best friend, etc. about your thoughts, ideas, and concerns regarding *piloting* the rest of YOUR life.

3. Make a list of specific actions you can take starting today to fuel your plane with more positive energy and with a focused direction.

   - Go to the companion website at **www.intentionallivinguniversity.com** for more articles, suggested books, video clips, etc.

Chapter 3

Balancing your Life Personally, Professionally and with Your Family: It's About Time!
"Keeping your plane flying smoothly and balanced"

As you pilot your plane and live your life, I am certain that you would want both *balanced*. Can you imagine if the bag handlers at the airport put all the luggage from the 100-200 passengers on one side of the plane? IF the plane could fly, it certainly would have to be flown differently. The same goes with your life. If your life is out of balance personally, professionally and with your family, you will always live compensating.

There are three important areas of one's life that need to be balanced to live well. First, your *personal* area which is inclusive of the eight dimensions of one's wellness: social, physical, emotional, career, intellectual, environmental, spiritual and financial. This also includes your ME time - making YOU a priority in your life.

Secondly, is your *professional* area which includes your job(s), career, volunteering hours and anything else you do as a profession. A minimum of one third of your entire life is hopefully *spent* here. Your profession should affect your entire life in a healthy, positive way.

The third area is *family.* This includes time with our own families who have nurtured and raised us, our children and their families and our in-laws or significant other's families. A finely tuned balance of these three areas is extremely important to our overall eventual happiness, satisfaction and life plan. Whether it be your immediate or your extended family - family is a huge part of our life that needs to be balanced. Many people neglect their families because they rationalize that they are providing for their family. Family time must be quality time with parents, grandparents, foster parents, mentors, etc. who are positive and healthy role models. Time spent with your family is simply priceless!

Balancing your life means growing and developing. Nobody is beyond growth. WE EITHER CONTINUE TO GROW OR BEGIN TO DIE. The choice and process of growing is a conscious and thoughtful paradigm shift.

Now is the time to seriously look at the life you are living, *the plane you are flying*. You need to check the *balance button* on the instrument panel. This calibrates how balanced your *flight pattern* is in your personal, professional and family lives.

I believe there are four ways to begin to balance your life, refocus and rejuvenate while planning your remaining years' *flight.*

- Closely look at and evaluate your life. Is there a balance in your personal, professional and family lives?
- Determine if your current employment not only provides the necessary income but the purpose and passion as well. You should feel you are making a positive impact within your line

of work. You ought to feel content and happy most days. If not, the tough decision of changing jobs might be the best interest for you AND your family.

- Begin to make daily plans that focus on your priorities.
- Write down your bucket list and post it where you can see it every day.

Balancing your life requires conscious thought and decision making regarding your priorities. This book will offer you the suggestions and opportunities that will guide you to balancing your life via a personal plan.

Think about your health, wellness and life from a *collective lifestyle* perspective. A *collective lifestyle* perspective involves enhancing your eight dimensions of wellness while intentionally balancing your personal, professional and family lives. These eight dimensions of one's wellness will be fully defined in more detail in the following chapter. The plan you develop will do just that; it will create a balance in your life according to your priorities including a focus on those eight dimensions of wellness.

Consider this quote, "The decisions we make now directly affect the quality of our future life and lifestyle." Do your priorities reflect the amount of time you spend with your family, your work and your personal goals? Do you intentionally plan to spend as much time as you can in each area? Ask yourself the following three questions:

- How do I want to spend the remaining time of my life?
- How can I better balance my life?
- What actions do I need to make to provide the balance I desire in my life?

As we consider balancing our lives for our priorities, we also need to realize that life is not a competition. It isn't about climbing that social ladder, making it into the million-dollar club, accumulating possessions, etc. It is about making relationships and memories. Balancing your life will allow for more of those memories to be made.

Looking at the research of many professional development gurus, I found five common threads that are keys to rejuvenation and more satisfaction in your life. These five keys are:

- Healing your wounds and celebrating your gifts.
- Managing your time for priorities.
- Integrating humor and laughter into your life.
- Intentionally choosing your attitude daily.
- Intentionally having more balance in your personal, professional, and family lives.

Balancing your life boils down to simply managing your time so that you are living for your priorities in all three areas, 24 hours a day, 7 days a week and 365 days a year. We only have 24 hours in a day. To become more balanced, you need to examine and prioritize the time you spend in your personal, professional and family lives. Daily time management is a skill that can be acquired and become a habit. Time has not changed. We need to prioritize and SPEND it differently. Steven Covey, professional development specialist and author of the national best-seller, *Seven Habits of Highly Effective People,* stated in his book, "Americans are the most time deprived people in the world. They have convinced themselves, that despite all of the high-tech, time-saving devices at their immediate disposal, they are doomed to terminal business." He also stated, "We get busier and busier doing good things and never really ask ourselves if WHAT we are doing matters MOST!"[1]

I believe that if you don't have enough time, you simply want too much! Not managing your time and balancing your life can lead to a lifestyle disease called *workaholism*. Many of you know workaholics. What a life. What a sad way to live. This lifestyle disease needs professional intervention and assistance. Physical, mental, emotional and social consequences will occur and drastically affect the overall wellness and balance in your life.

I have a confession to make as I write this book. I am a recovering workaholic. My life as a passionate educator, coach, speaker, basketball official, part-time dad was simply out of control for 18 years. I had come to a realization that I was a workaholic and my life was completely out of balance. I remember the relief I felt when I finally realized I had the "disease" of workaholism. Why did I eventually feel relief? I finally identified this characteristic and was willing to change and do something about it.

This chapter is about intentional life balance. As a pilot, your wings represent the three areas of your life. If the wings are not balanced according to your *dashboard instrument,* you need to adjust. Just as in life when those areas of your life are not balanced, you must *correct.* There is no auto-correct, no auto-pilot in our lives. YOU must initiate the change. If not, you will start drifting toward an undetermined and possibly an unwanted destination. A pilot flying an aircraft is in control of the wing balance. While in training, pilots are repeatedly told by their instructors to *trim up* and find their *center.* Likewise, it is with us; we need to find our *center in life.* Our center is our plan that provides us the necessary balance in our lives.

First and foremost, true life balance is about taking the necessary time for YOU! Yes, you first. What an unthinkable idea. Why *you* first? Not only because it's usually you who is last on the time allocation chart, but without the necessary personal time for self-care, energy attainment and proper attitude, the other two areas of life are directly affected. You simply will not be as effective as a professional, colleague, parent or spouse.

Would you like: more energy, less stress at home, less stress at your job, more opportunities for fun, more time for your priorities, more passion for the things that motivate you, more opportunities to live happier than you already may be, and live longer with a more quality lifestyle? If so, YOU must make yourself a priority. That may be difficult, but it is critically necessary. This could mean relieving yourself of some duties, saying "no" more often or simply withdrawing from activities that are monopolizing your time, etc.

For the balance equation to occur, it is strongly suggested that you begin to clear your daily schedule in life and make time for your new number one priority, which NEEDS to be YOU. I know the guilt trip will creep in. You could let that battle be conquered by your guilt causing nothing to change, or you can begin to understand that it is imperative to care for yourself first and foremost, so you can be that effective employee, colleague, loving spouse or parent. YOU need to be listed in your top 5 priorities in life. If not, I challenge you to begin that journey, that process, that scheduling of time for YOU in your daily calendar or on your TO DO list. This is critical to providing more balance in your personal life.

We need to fill ourselves up with the required energy by exercising, relaxing and doing the things we enjoy, so we can care more effectively for our spouse, our children, our biological family, the people we serve and our colleagues at work. Many of us take such poor care of our own needs and desires that we end up in a constant state of stress, frustration, fatigue and overall poor mental and physical health. We need to start prioritizing our time *beginning with ourselves*.

Let's begin by looking at our normal 24-hour day. Within the twenty-four hours of each day, most of us sleep on an average of eight hours a day. If you live to be sixty-years-of-age, you will have slept for twenty years! Yes, twenty years! I suggest having a comfortable mattress that provides restful sleep if you are going to sleep one-third of your life in it! Most of us spend approximately 8-10 hours a day working and commuting. That leaves approximately 6-8 hours a day for OURSELVES, our spouse or significant other, our communities and our families. Most often, your work-life is what is needed to financially survive. We spend the majority of our lives working 30, 40, 50, maybe even 60 YEARS! Given that perspective, your time spent with your work is critical to your life balance.

—

36

Are you spending the majority of your time in your life with your career? Realize your work normally takes at least 8-9 hours of our priceless day most every day. It's extremely important to enjoy your work, be happy in it and have it in balance with the REST of your life. Consider this quote, *"Choose a job you love and you will never have to work a day in your life" (Confucius)*. If the job you have isn't making you happy and doesn't allow for life balance, consider changing it. Seriously! It may be difficult, but it also may be one of the best decisions you will ever make for YOU, your spouse, your family and possibly for the new employer! No one on their death bed has expressed, "I wished I would have spent more time at work." These may be the times in your life where you realize that income and benefits need to have less of an emphasis which may include an entire career change.

To help in this area of your life, start by asking yourself the following questions:
- Do you feel like you are needed at your place of employment?
- Do you feel like you are making some difference?
- Does your work give you energy?
- Does your work directly affect your attitude in a positive way?
- Do you feel your work is important to your style of living?
- Are you spending too much of your life with your work?
- What is it that has you staying in this field?
- Will this career provide you the passion needed in your life?
- Does this career allow you to balance your life?

Many employees I speak to and train are beginning to choose and make their VOCATION A VACATION while being professional and doing their job well. It is an ATTITUDE - a different perspective. Assessing this portion of your life is critical to finding balance, happiness and satisfaction.

Now let's look at the time we spend with our families including our spouse or significant other. First, we need to define what constitutes quality family time. Simply taking family members to their activities and watching their involvement does not constitute quality family time. What does then? Quality time depends on what your family deems important: communication, social interaction, activities, etc. Are you spending quality time on a planned schedule when possible? Does YOUR daily TO-DO calendar reflect quality family time on a regular basis? Is this something that needs to be brought into balance?

The following story reinforces the importance of spending quality time with family.

A dad came home from work late and very, very tired and extremely irritated with the day's activities. As he opened the door to his house, he found his six-year-old son patiently waiting for him. The young boy gave his dad a heart-warming hug, and then blurted, "Daddy, can I ask you a question?"

"Yeah, sure," replied the father.

"Daddy, how much do you make in an hour?"

"That's really none of your business, Son! Why do you have to know how much I make? Why would you ask such a thing?" he angrily questioned.

"I just wanna know! Please, Daddy, how much money do you make an hour?" pleaded the little boy. After thinking a bit, the father eventually replied, "If you must know, I make about $20.00 an hour."

"Ohhhhh," the son immediately replied with a saddened face and bowed his head. Slowly looking back up at his dad, he asked, "Daddy, may I borrow $10.00 please?"

The father became angry and said, "If the only reason you want $10.00 is so you can go buy some silly toy or something that you don't need, then march yourself to your bedroom. Think about what you just asked for and think about your selfishness! And before you go to bed, think about the long, hard hours I work each and every day to pay the bills.

———

I come home late and then continue to work until I'm too tired to stay up any longer. And in the morning, I start all over again. I just don't know why you would even ask for $10.00 for your selfish desires!"

The son quietly dragged his feet with his head down and went to his bedroom and shut the door. The dad sat down and angrily contemplated about his son's request. After an hour or so, he began to calm down and started to think that maybe he had been a little too hard on his son. Just maybe there was something his son needed or was saving for that was very important to him. His son rarely asked for money.

The dad went to his son's bedroom and quietly opened the door. "Are you still up, Son?" he asked.

"Yes, Daddy, I'm awake," he immediately replied as he sat up.

Dad sat on the edge of his bed. "I've been thinking, Son, that maybe I was a little too harsh on you when I came home from work and you asked me those questions about how much money I make. It has been another very long day and I'm really sorry I took out my frustrations and aggravations on you. Here's that $10.00 you asked for."

The little boy beamed with a smile from ear to ear. "Oh, thank you Daddy!" he exclaimed while hugging his dad. Then the son reached under his pillow. He pulled out a few more crumpled up bills.

Dad became frustrated and angry once again. "Why did you need $10.00 when you already have some money?" he asked.

The son slowly counted his money as his father continued to grumble. "Because," he said, "I didn't have enough money before, but now I do. Daddy, I have $20.00 now. Can I buy one hour of your time?"

———

Enough said about the true value and need for quality family time! We race around busier and busier each day thinking we are providing for our children when all they really want is our TIME! Plan to balance your family life with a focused emphasis of quality time. One needs to consider not only the amount of time but whether it is quality time. Does your present daily calendar express a focus on family time? Is that a priority of yours? If so, why isn't it planned for daily, by intention, within your daily TO DO list? Enjoy the time brainstorming with your spouse and your children incorporating planned daily, weekly, monthly or yearly QUALITY family times. Remember, most kids spell LOVE.... TIME!

Some people plan their lives like packing a suitcase. Some roll each article of clothing to get more clothes to fit into the suitcase. Some people intentionally plan to get more to fit into their day. Just like my wife, who rolls all her clothing as she packs her suitcase to travel, we need to plan to make things such as family, friends, spouses, your significant other *fit* into our daily lives.

What can you do to take action to better balance your life? Let's begin with the personal area first since it IS the most important!

PERSONAL LIFE
**Write something YOU are going to do for YOU on your daily TO DO list every day. NO GUILT-none-nadda!

PHYSICAL
- Exercise
- Pray
- Massage
- Read
- Salon
- Hobby
- Shop

PROFESSIONAL LIFE

**Try and leave your work at work with a specific daily TO-DO list and stick to It!

- CHOOSE to make at least one day a week a happy and positively infectious one. MONDAY? THURSDAY?
- Find a way to have fun and enjoy yourself while working.
- Put the things that bother you and people who stress you at work into perspective.
- Be grateful at work and find the time to personally thank 3-5 people who you appreciate working with.
- Concentrate on how fortunate you are to have a job when things start getting you down at work.

FAMILY LIFE

**Examine the time you spend on your personal self, with work and with your family. Then make a concerted effort to spend more quality family time and add it in onto your daily TO DO list. If family is a priority, put those events and activities on your daily TO DO list FIRST.

- Exercise together.
- Plan a family night.
- Plan for family stress management time.
- Plan family mealtimes more often. If at all possible, intentionally plan for a minimum of three family meals a week.

You must come to the realization that balancing your life comes down to managing your time and priorities. Management of time needs to include you first, your spouse, family and then your job – IN THAT ORDER! Most of you reading this book have another twenty to forty years left to live. I encourage you to seriously think about how you want to "spend your time" with YOU – chosen as a priority during those remaining years. How do you begin the process of making this happen, making this a habit and fully incorporating this into your life? I challenge you to begin by using my daily TO DO list for 7-14 days.

Intentionally Constructed Daily TO-DO List

REMINDERS

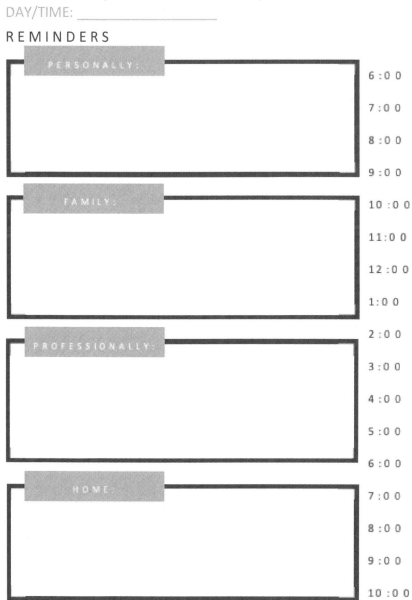

PERSONALLY:

FAMILY:

PROFESSIONALLY:

HOME:

6:00

7:00

8:00

9:00

10:00

11:00

12:00

1:00

2:00

3:00

4:00

5:00

6:00

7:00

8:00

9:00

10:00

One thing I am grateful for today is...

One thing I can do today to "Pay It Forward" is...

One person I intend to make a difference with today is...

After writing all your appointments and tasks you have to do along the right side next to the desired specific time, also write them in one of the appropriate boxes on the left. Be diligent in writing EVERYTHING you are planning to do. Staple each day to the previous days' sheets. After 7-14 days, take a serious look at how you are spending your time. Ask yourself: Is my life balanced personally, professionally and with my family? Am I listed as a priority to do the necessary and critical personal things for me first? Do you find revelations that lead you to realize your life needs to be more balanced? Then, with intention, each day plan small changes to aid in the balance of your personal, professional and family lives. Each week plan for some more consistent changes with the balancing of your time - your life! It will be very clear where you need to start. The sky is the limit for options to change. Enjoy creating those new plans, those new focused intentions, especially the ones involving time for YOU! Remember, happy and successful people don't find time when they can, they MAKE time daily by intention and with a purpose.

So, how do we do that? It is all about intentional planning for the things one wants to do that provides a balance in one's life. Feel free to make more copies of the daily TO DO list. Start planning your days with more intention, looking at the 4 daily areas (personal, professional, family and home) while focusing on and giving attention to your priorities.   After all, "Life is not measured by the number of breaths we take but by the number of moments that take our breath away." Plan for those breathless moments as you intentionally plan to live for your priorities in a balanced life.

As you read this book and begin to implement some of the suggestions, hopefully you should find that:

- You have more energy.
- You have less stress at home and with your job.
- You have more opportunities for fun.
- You have more time for your priorities.
- You have more passion for the things that motivate you.
- You have more opportunities to live happier.
- You make better wellness choices to live a long, QUALITY of life.

I sincerely believe that by intentionally balancing your life you will begin to reap many, if not all, of these benefits. While you continue to pilot your plane, *live your life*, realize that NOW you have more tools to live healthier in all eight dimensions and more balanced in the three areas discussed. Find the necessary energy and the needed attitude to TRULY LIVE while you thoroughly ENJOY YOUR NEXT 30-60 YEARS!

Continue to fly and keep your plane balanced for everyone's sake while you enjoy your ride. Your life flight plan should include a conscious focus intentionally allowing balance in your life. Most importantly balance in your personal life, then within your family and finally professionally. I challenge you to intentionally prioritize YOU first when adopting your flight plan.

As the pilot of the rest of your life, fly your plane/live your life in balance. A smooth, balanced ride is a good ride. If "gusty winds" intermittently disrupt your life balance, return to a "higher altitude" and find balance by your choice and design.

SAFE FLIGHT CHECKLIST:

- Intentionally and daily try and balance your life personally, professionally and with your family.
- Realize the decisions you make today affect the quality of your life in the future.
- Utilize a daily "To Do" list to observe how you "spend" the majority of your time. Then adjust accordingly.

YOUR FLIGHT ACTION PLAN:

1. Use the TO-DO list for 7-14 days to schedule your daily activities. Review this list after the seven days. Make *flight* and life corrections. Make your own personal TO-DO list.
2. As you put your head on your pillow each night for a minimum of seven days, simply ask yourself, "Did I live a balanced day today?" Adjust your next day accordingly.

3. Stand on one leg for as long as possible. What happens? Compare your life to your body on one leg and predict what might occur if you had limited balance. Then make your *flight alterations* or life changes.

4. Intentionally choose to slow down and live more balanced *one day at a time.* Much like a recovering alcoholic or drug addict has to live each of their days one day at a time.

   - Go to the companion website at **www.intentionallivinguniversity.com** for more articles, suggested books, video clips, etc.

Chapter 4

Assessing the Eight Dimensions of Your Wellness
"Consciously living WELL while you are flying"

How do you respond when someone asks you, "How are you?" Usually the response is automatic, "I'm good, I'm well, I'm pretty good," "not too bad", or "I'm okay." Most of the time your brain responds to the condition of your physical health. You deduce quickly, "I'm not physically sick, so I must be well." How do you know if you are really well? Not just physically, but mentally, emotionally, socially, intellectually, environmentally, career-wise, spiritually and financially? These areas should definitely be considered when determining your total wellness, not just your physical health. Consider this metaphor to give you a better understanding of your true wellness. Again, you are the pilot flying the plane. There are eight *pre-checks* that the control tower radios to the co-pilot and then to you BEFORE you begin this flight. These are items with the plane that must be in sound working condition before you can take off and have a safe flight and eventual landing. Similarly, your life has eight *pre-checks* or wellness dimensions. These dimensions have to be in sound working order to live a healthy, happy and successful life. If one is out of order, the plane could be *grounded.* If one wellness dimension is out of order in your life, it directly affects the seven others. If you try to live a life where you are not truly well; it is hard to get off the ground. It is difficult to fly, difficult to live happily and difficult to die with no regrets.

As the pilot, you sit at the gate and look out at your plane. Then you begin to walk around the entire plane checking for anything that is not normal such as nicks, low tire pressure, bent flaps, etc. This as a visual check to look for anything specifically out of the ordinary that needs attention. Being the pilot, the pilot of your life, it is important to check your *plane* or all your eight dimensions of wellness BEFORE you fly.

This chapter explains each dimension of wellness in detail so you can *go through your own pre-check* to determine the state of your total wellness and begin to take specific actions with the dimensions you feel you need to develop and improve in your life. First of all, let me define "wellness." Wellness is more than the absence of disease and symptoms. Wellness can be defined as the pursuit of a WELL and BALANCED lifestyle. It involves finding a healthy balance of the mind, body and spirit which results in an overall satisfied and content feeling. It also involves choosing behaviors and making decisions that are healthy, legal and safe.

By intentionally being more WELL overall, you can:
- Decrease risks for both contagious and lifestyle diseases.
- Prevent rapid aging and premature death.
- Increase your life satisfaction, contentment and happiness.
- Live with more balance - personally, professionally and with your family.
- Increase the quality of your life
- Intentionally plan for a long life with few regrets.
- Live a life that is well-planned with intention and purpose.

The eight dimensions of wellness overlap and synergistically work together. One wellness dimension can have a direct influence on each of the other seven. When all dimensions are consciously thought about, developed and enhanced, one will readily begin not

---

only to feel differently but live differently. Wellness is an ongoing process of making choices towards a healthier and more fulfilling life. Your wellness lifestyle comes down to making healthy, legal and safe CHOICES - those that contribute to your overall quality of life.

So, what are these eight flight *pre-checks*? The eight dimensions of a person's life include:

SOCIAL WELLNESS: The process of creating and maintaining healthy relationships through the interactions we have with others.

Social wellness also deals with access to support, whether in health, legal, and economic areas. It is somewhat correlated to our socio-economic status. Actually, research has shown that incarcerations, negative health outcomes and drop-out rates can be connected to one's zip code. Social status and wealth impact social wellness. Social wellness is about acquiring the necessary skills to maintain and improve relationships. Additionally, your EQ (emotional quotient) is important with your social wellness-just as important as your IQ (intelligence quotient).

Possible actions to take to improve this dimension:

- Get out of toxic relationships you may be in.
- Strengthen the relationships you have with a communal conscious effort.
- Check your EQ-emotional quotient and begin working on being more emotionally intelligent.
- Set yourself up more often with small groups of people.
- Tell the people you have a strong, sincere and healthy relationship with that they are appreciated.
- Introduce yourself to people you don't know with confidence.
- Visit other cultures.
- Smile often-be infectious with your positive attitude.
- Travel and be with other people.
- Be more empathetic.
- Confidently connect with three people a month at work that you don't know very well.

- Plan more experiences with people.
- Establish more friendships if you would like more.
- Be a good listener.
- Work on your communication with people.
- Identify how others may perceive you.
- Work on the small things that make a difference.
- Identify what you like in others who are social and work on a few of those characteristics.
- Balance your alone time with family, spouse and friends.
- Do for others and help whenever and wherever you can, especially in times of need.
- Etc.

PHYSICAL/PERSONAL WELLNESS: The process of making choices that create strong minds and bodies. Those choices are primarily and directly related to self-care, exercise, nutrition, weight management, sleep and stress management. Physical wellness deals with issues including obesity. According to data collected by the Center for Disease Control (CDC), 39.5% of the American population is considered obese and that trend is alarmingly increasing. Obesity is a major risk factor for a myriad of diseases, diabetes and cardio-vascular disease being two of the most serious. Physical wellness also deals with your diet and exercise which can minimize and prevent several deleterious effects on your body. This dimension of wellness also deals with negative body images that is oftentimes contrary to healthy guidelines and realistic physical images. Understanding both contagious and lifestyle diseases and their prevention is a major aspect in the physical wellness dimension as well.

Possible actions to take to improve this dimension:

- Exercise.
- Floss.
- Meditate.
- Eat four smaller meals a day.

- Eat less sugar.
- Quit smoking, chewing tobacco, vaping to reduce nicotine.
- Stop or reduce soda consumption.
- Eat more colored vegetables.
- Eat less red meat.
- Reduce carbohydrates.
- Reduce salt intake.
- Have an annual physical.
- Relax more often.
- Appreciate the moment more often.
- Treat yourself regularly to a massage, pedicure, manicure, etc.
- Gain, maintain or lose weight in a healthy way.
- Eat less fatty, greasy or fried foods.
- Wear sunscreen.
- Wear seatbelt and motorcycle helmet.
- Reduce alcohol consumption.
- Quit the "social use" of illegal drugs.
- Focus on a lifestyle disease that you are prone to acquire and its prevention.
- Wash hands more often. Try and wash them at least eight times a day.
- Drink more water- especially before meals if trying to lose weight (up to half of your body weight in ounces).
- Practice personal stress management techniques and coping strategies before you become or when you are feeling stressed.
- Etc.

MENTAL/EMOTIONAL WELLNESS: The process of the way we think, accepting our worth, creating, recognizing and expressing our feelings in healthy ways while moving towards self-actualization. Mental and emotional health includes both our psychological and emotional welfare. Poor mental and emotional health can lead to loss of social support, jobs and potentially your life. As you are probably aware, mental illness is a growing concern in the United

---

States and must be given the necessary attention across all age levels. Identifying and treating mental illness can be challenging and can be very taxing on your friends, family and loved ones. It is important that we recognize the difference between mental health and mental illness. Regarding mental illness, knowing the causes, symptoms, and how to receive help is critical.

Possible actions to take to improve this dimension:

- Admit you may need help and seek professional guidance- that's a very healthy thing to do.
- Share feelings more often and in constructive ways.
- Avoid negative self-talk.
- Find your passions, identify your priorities and plan for them daily.
- Plan for more happy experiences in your day.
- Cope with depression in healthy, legal and safe ways.
- Love deeper - show it - say it and mean it.
- Accept yourself with all of your perfections and possible imperfections.
- Get your needs met in healthy ways - the need of love, acceptance, touch, etc.
- Keep your mind sharp.
- Identify the many ways of being more mentally and emotionally well and practice those behaviors until they become habits.
- Trust.
- Forgive.
- Heal past wounds such as divorce, separation and abuse.
- Let go.
- Practice mindfulness.
- Be a life-long learner.
- Re-connect with friends or family members that you need to forgive.
- Etc.

CAREER/OCCUPATIONAL WELLNESS: The process of making and maintaining choices related to work including working in a place for which one is well suited and enjoys. Career/Occupational wellness is the process of enriching your life through a career choice or volunteer work. It is about finding personal satisfaction in what you do for a living since it encompasses a significant amount of our time. When we love what we do, we find purpose and meaning for our lives. Another aspect of career/occupational wellness is finding balance between work and leisure time. Our society often pressures people to work more than to relax, which has led to an epidemic in chronic stress.

Possible actions to take to improve this dimension:

- Choose a job that you thoroughly enjoy.
- Intentionally plan to be a professional while still having fun in the process.
- Make your vocation a vacation, while still being professional.
- Thank your colleagues.
- If in a leadership role, regularly and sincerely thank your employees.
- If you are in a career going nowhere and you are unhappy, try and secure another assignment or find another job.
- Realize that the best job doesn't necessarily correlate to the best pay.
- Thank your supervisor or boss sincerely.
- Give 110% and you will reap many side benefits at other times.
- Balance your job with your personal and family life.
- Understand what workaholism is and avoid getting caught in that addictive condition.
- Deal as best you can with those people who make work difficult.
- Etc.

INTELLECTUAL WELLNESS: The process of using our minds to create a greater understanding and appreciation of the world as well as being an active life-long learner. Intellectual wellness is a life-long process and is primarily a self-directed pursuit. Oftentimes, we mistake intellect to be primarily our experiences in educational institutions. In this era of overwhelming data and alternative facts, our intellect is important for everyone to be able to discern what is factual, what is accurate and what is personally useful. Intellectual wellness involves critical thinking, learning and your memory. Cognitive diseases such as dementia and Alzheimer's can affect your intellectual wellness. Mental illness may also have a direct effect on this dimension of wellness.

Possible actions to take to improve this dimension:
- Read.
- Take a class to learn something new.
- Contemplate more often.
- Read more.
- Dream daily and turn some of those into plans.
- Plan to learn something new every day.
- Identify your best learning strategies.
- Choose a new hobby every year or two.
- Utilize your intellectual talents for services or volunteering.
- Play trivia games with Alexa, the Dot or on your computer.
- Do puzzles that continue to stimulate the brain-newspaper-phone apps-puzzle books-etc.
- Etc.

ENVIRONMENTAL WELLNESS: The process of making choices which will contribute to sustaining and improving the quality of life on our earth including our air, water and land quality. This dimension involves improving your standard of living by creating healthy surroundings in your environment, as well as several areas outside of it. Environmental wellness includes not only pollution prevention and recycling, but also assessing what toxins lurk in our everyday life as well. It also about making your surroundings safe which includes abuse prevention. It may even involve personal decisions that affect others around you such as alcohol and drug abuse, not wearing your seatbelt, texting while driving, etc.

Possible actions to take to improve this dimension:
- Recycle.
- Shorter showers.
- Decide not to let water run when brushing your teeth.
- Make a compost pile.
- Pick up garbage when you see it.
- Use environmentally friendly lawn and garden products.
- Buy water efficient toilets.
- Put a container of 32 ounces of liquid in the toilet tank - you will use less each flush.
- Buy products with less packaging.
- Purchase home cleaning products that are more natural with less chemicals and toxins.
- Purchase shampoos and make-up that are more natural with less chemicals and toxins.
- Avoid situations of abuse.
- If you have been abused in ANY way, do something constructive to begin the healing process so you can move on.
- Drink alcohol in moderation.
- Take prescriptions with recommended instructions IF needed.
- Take any unused or unwanted prescriptions to "take-back" centers.
- Avoid any drug abuse.
- Decide not to drive buzzed, drunk or "in-texticated" (driving while texting).
- Decide not to ride with someone who has been drinking, is buzzed, drunk or texts while driving.
- Etc.

SPIRITUAL WELLNESS: The process of finding and living a meaningful and purposeful life through a belief system while demonstrating those values through specific behaviors. Spiritual wellness approaches have been shown to be an integral part of the healthy self. However, there has been a blurring of the lines at times when it comes to the differences between spirituality and religion. More recently health care teams incorporate spiritual assistance such as chaplains, ministers, priests, meditation and laugh therapy, just to name a few. Spiritual wellness may include a faith, a belief in core values, a hope, an anticipation, a reflection, an after-life awareness or having a purpose.

Possible actions to take to improve this dimension:

- Identify what your basic core values are and start to live them by intentional planning.
- Identify your core belief system about why and how you live.
- Find your spiritual self.
- Decide to strengthen your Faith.
- Decide to do more for the place you worship than you do.
- Make an intentional effort to set aside time daily to pray or meditate.
- Meditate more often.
- Practice mindfulness with a spiritual focus.
- Identify your purpose in life.
- Live for your purpose with daily intentional planning.
- Read the Bible or similar religious readings.
- Go to a place of worship more often.
- Etc.

FINANCIAL WELLNESS: The process of consciously being aware of and developing a money system that comforts you and meets both your needs and wants.

Financial wellness deals with how you budget money and prepare for the future so that you have less anxiety about money. Financial stress directly impacts your physical, mental and social health. Financial wellness helps you learn how to successfully manage money and explore programs that can assist you with your unique financial needs.

Possible actions to take to improve this dimension:

- Meet with a financial counselor despite your money situation.
- Invest when and if you can. Set aside a decided amount of money per month for your eventual retirement - have a certain amount automatically deducted from your pay check if you can and deposited directly into an account for retirement.
- Grocery shop when you are full to avoid binge buying.
- Cut coupons-look for sales.
- Begin to realize that money isn't everything.
- Realize if you are healthy-you are wealthy.
- Shop around for insurances.
- Decide if life insurance fits your needs.
- Pay off your loans ASAP.
- Establish credit for when you need a loan. If you use a credit card, pay it off monthly - no exceptions.
- Avoid using credit cards when and if you can.
- Budget your monthly income and be frugal.
- Take advantage of all employee financial benefits.
- Etc.

So, how well are you now? Are you flying the plane, *living your life* with those *pre-checks* running efficiently? Wouldn't it be interesting if we had a *warning light* go off in our lives when one of our wellness dimensions started to go haywire? This danger light would make us readily aware that we are not well within that dimension and we would need to do something to correct our flight, *life* before it affected our entire *descent*. I challenge you to intentionally live well. Feel content. Feel good. Feel alive. Feel happier. LIVE!

Pilots live by *pre-checks and check lists;* we should also! Assessing our eight dimensions of wellness and then intermittently checking them on a regular basis is crucial to our *flight.* You may have to "go outside" and check your *plane* as pilots do. Once in the cockpit, pilots have many things to check including pre-start checks, starting checks, before take-off checks, after take-off checks, climb checks, cruise checks, descent checks, approach checks, before landing checks, after landing checks and finally shutdown checks. Our lives require as many checks as we live our *plan.*

Your wellness is an investment, not an expense. Start investing today for the rest of your life. It can be done with little effort. Remember our wellness is like money. We never have a true idea of its value until we lose it. Be a priority; fall in love with taking care of yourself - your own wellness. It WILL have a ripple effect on all those around you. Quite often we don't really know how good our body is designed to feel. As with nutrition, we must nourish to flourish. The same goes for your wellness. Nourish your eight dimensions. Feel the change. Let today be the start of that nourishment, your new life, your *descent.* It is critical to understand that it is never too late to work towards being the "WELL-thiest" you!

SAFE FLIGHT CHECKLIST:

- Assess yourself in all 8 of the dimensions of wellness.
- Know specific actions you can take in each dimension that will make you more WELL.
- Start investing in your wellness by infusing those behaviors into your life's mission plan.

YOUR FLIGHT ACTION PLAN:

1. Assess yourself in the eight dimensions of wellness. There are many on-line versions.
2. Choose a dimension for each month and make a list of relevant and attainable behaviors that you can take to be more well within that dimension. After the eighth month, start over. Post your behaviors on your bathroom mirror or screensaver each month.

3. Choose to make yourself a priority starting today, so you can be a more loving spouse and parent, a more caring friend, as well as a more effective employee. Write yourself in your daily planner and BECOME a priority.

4. Realize each day is truly a gift. Yesterday is gone. Tomorrow isn't here yet. Graciously take today as a GIFT. Unwrap it and use it to live with intention, passion and with purpose. This is why they call today the PRESENT! Take care of your gift each day by choosing one aspect of wellness and integrating it into your life until it becomes a habit.

   - Go to the companion website at **www.intentionallivinguniversity.com** for more articles, suggested books, video clips, etc.

.

Chapter 5

Choosing the Attitude that YOU Want for the Day

"Intentionally flying and positively 'infecting' everyone on board"

"Please fasten your seatbelts and take a mere ten seconds to choose the attitude you want for the *rest of the flight.*" Once again, you are the pilot of your life and you are in full control comfortably in the cockpit. Let's check your ADI-your Attitude Detection Indicator. The effects of attitude and its overall effect on your entire being deserves a great deal of explanation.

Why not start each day with the attitude you have chosen for the day. A brief, conscious thought process in the morning and sometimes intermittently throughout your day will make for a better flight- *a happier life.* This attitude may come with a different perspective, more energy and satisfaction. It should be infectious to others. If you don't choose your attitude daily, others will choose and shape it for you. It might be your spouse, kids, colleagues, clients or random others. Don't you want to be the one who chooses your daily attitude? If so, you need to consciously choose the attitude you want every day.

Our universe is made of energy. Einstein taught us that. One doesn't need to think deeply about science to understand life is all about energy. Just think about your own life. Think about the people that increase or decrease your energy. Think about the foods that increase or decrease your energy. Think about the personal or business projects that increase or decrease your energy. Really, everything revolves around energy. Our thoughts are powerful because they are loaded with energy. Remember, if you want to change your outlook, you must change your attitude and your thoughts; both are forms of energy.

"It's a good day to have a good day!" This is a perfect quote to start your day. It is fairly easy to consciously decide each morning that it is going to be a good day and then remind yourself throughout the day. Result? It becomes a good day and quite often the day gets even better with our intermittent attitude reminders. You all remember, Willard Scott, the meteorologist that regularly interviewed centenarians and made commercials for Smucker's Jelly. One day he was interviewing a lady at the young age of 103. He asked her what her top three secrets were to a long, healthy life. She immediately responded, "Attitude. Having a positive attitude is key to a healthy life."

Attitude was her initial response. How has your attitude been recently? How is it today? How about right now? Have you consciously thought of the attitude you would like for today? What about the one you would like for tomorrow? Choosing your daily attitude is as crucial as brushing your teeth or taking a shower. In fact, when doing those mindless activities, they are a perfect time to think about the attitude you desire for the day.

What specifically is attitude? It is a blend of the way we think and how we feel. It's shaped and set daily; one way or another. It

---

changes if WE consciously let it change. It stays on the forefront of our minds if we train it to do so. Starting your day with a thought-process for your attitude, I believe is CRITICAL to your happiness, success and maybe even to your business. "Dress yourself" daily with an attitude of your choice. Once again, if you choose not to, you are allowing circumstances and others to choose an attitude for you.

Your attitude is quite evident. It is something other people can actually see. They can hear it in your voice. They can sense it while you work. They can see it in your body language. It is expressed in EVERYTHING you do, ALL of the time, wherever you are at home, at work or in your personal life. Your choice of attitude each and every day is very important whether that is realized by you or not.

Your daily attitude is important; it is more important than:
- the past
- your intelligence or past education
- money
- circumstances
- past successes or failures
- what others think, say or do
- your appearance
- giftedness
- your talents and skills

We can't change our past. We can't change the fact that people will act in a certain way. We can't change the inevitable. Life is 10% what happens to YOU and 90% how YOU REACT to it. Convince yourself: WE ARE IN CHARGE OF OUR ATTITUDES. Mary Englebeit from www.organizemyhouse.com states, "If you don't like something, change it. If you can't change it, change the way you think about it." Think about this quote. *A negative attitude is like a flat tire. You can't go anywhere until you change it.* Your attitude shapes the potential for a healthy functioning self-esteem, creativity, insight, wisdom, ability to unconditionally love, have healthy relationships, motivation, ability to laugh, problem-solve and of course, your overall optimism.

Ask yourself intermittently, "Is my attitude right now appealing to others?" To start this attitude-change process, I'd like to suggest that you to try going 12-24 hours without complaining about anything. Focus on your positive attitude when you feel the urge to complain. Choose a day and just TRY IT. You WILL be amazed! I believe that you can alter your LIFE simply by altering your daily attitude by engaging in the *intentional thought-process.* No matter how good or bad your life may be right now, wake up each morning and be thankful you can and that you still have one. Look in the mirror each morning and say, "I can do this, and I'll do it with a positive attitude." Begin intentionally choosing your attitude each morning as part of your daily routine.

Think about this question: *What do YOU wake up FOR everyday?* Your thoughts should bring a positive attitude that is affirming and uplifting. Vince Lombardi, legendary coach of the Green Bay Packers, once said, "Changes made by your body can be made fairly simply. Changes made by your mind are a lot more difficult, but a lot more rewarding!" Remember, GOOD VIBES IN - GOOD ACTIONS OUT, BAD VIBES IN- BAD ACTIONS OUT. Or another way of phrasing it, GARBAGE IN – GARBAGE OUT. In essence, what consumes your mind, controls your life. Start thinking positively and see how your world changes. Some people have a condition coined C.A.P.S. - Cranial Anal Personality Syndrome. One's attitude has a negative view which affects their environment, their relationships and their overall life. In order to have a positive attitude, you must have charisma; that is having the ability to get along with others, communicate effectively and have a sense of positivity about you that makes others want to be around you. Charisma - you can't buy it - you can't make it and you certainly can't fake it. Try not to suffer from what we call "psycho-attitude-sclerosis," a hardening of the attitudes. The condition is contagious! You know the people that have this condition. They, however, may unfortunately not know it.

There are two types of people in this world. Those people who brighten up the room whenever they enter it, and those people who brighten up the room whenever they leave it. Your attitude is often contingent upon the gratitude in your life. Dr. Norman Cousins, a noted writer and researcher on health and wellness issues, suggests 10-15 minutes a day should be set aside for daily reflection, giving thanks, prayer or meditation. He feels it is as important as physical exercise. Start a daily gratitude journal to aid in this process.[2] Our happiness, which is attained from our passions, is directly related to our attitude. Happiness, gratefulness and attitude are intertwined and definitely affect each other in many ways.

Worrying also has a definite effect on our attitude. *Anxiety does not empty tomorrow of its sorrow, but only empties today of our strength.* Research clearly demonstrates that an average worrier is 92% inefficient. Only 8% of what we worry about ever comes true! I have a great suggestion for fingernail biters: CHANGE YOUR WORRYING TIMES TO WISHING TIMES OR PRAYING TIMES. Your brain simply cannot do both simultaneously! As far as your negative talk goes, tell the negative committee that meets inside your head *to sit down and shut up!* According to Wayne Dyer, a health guru and motivational speaker and trainer, *what we resist persists.*

Quite often we attract what we fear throughout our day, week, month or year. Focusing on the positives in your day or life is a much healthier way to live. Often, people have too many subconscious negative attitude infectors. Subconscious or subliminal attitudes often creep in even with positive attitudes. For example, how many of you have ever said, "Thank God It's Friday"? Well, unless you had something planned for that weekend, your Monday, Tuesday, Wednesday, and Thursday must have really stunk! TGIF has become so commonplace that I am sure you have seen the restaurant chain named after it. TGFT is the attitude that is much needed. Thank God for Today! Again, being grateful and thankful consciously and regularly every day helps shape our attitudes.

As you well know, we all have issues in our lives. We all have some type of cross to bear. But even when you have pains, you don't have to be one! The fact that you have been given another day, should be exciting!

Also, our attitude gets a whole lot better if we put things into perspective. How about this quote regarding attitude? *People who wonder whether the glass is half full or half empty miss the point. The glass is refillable!*

There is a story called "A Woman and Her Hair" that speaks volumes about attitude and perspective.

There once was a woman dealing with chemotherapy and cancer. She woke up one morning, looked in the mirror and noticed she had only three hairs left on her head. "Well," she said, "I think I'll braid my hair today!" So, she did and she continued to enjoy a wonderful day.

The next day she woke up again, looked in the mirror and saw that she had only two hairs left on her head. "H-M-M-M," she said, "I think I'll part my hair down the middle today." So, she did and she had a grand day!

The next day she woke up, looked in the mirror and noticed she had only one hair left on her head. "Well," she said, "Today I'm going to wear my hair in a ponytail." So, she did and had an absolutely fabulous day!

Attitude IS everything and sometimes the crosses we are forced to bear are life altering. Yet we must keep them in perspective. Yes, losing your hair due to cancer may be tragic. But in perspective, losing your hair is better than losing your life.

Have you ever let one little thing affect your attitude and completely ruin your entire day? Deciphering between

---

66

inconveniences and problems is also critical to your daily attitude. When was the last time you let a small inconvenience damage your entire day, weekend or portion of your trip? I was speaking to a group of employees about this very topic and a lady raised her hand and asked if she could share her story where she learned this valuable life lesson.

Linda was from a small town in northwest Wisconsin. She rarely traveled. She actually had never left the state of Wisconsin in all her years. Her sister, Carol, who lived in New York invited her to visit. Linda reluctantly agreed. The plane ride was nerve-wracking. The airport was stressful, but when she finally saw Carol at the baggage claim, she felt extremely relieved and at home again. On the way to Carol's house, Carol explained to Linda that she unexpectedly got called back to work. Carol suggested that Linda take some time to explore Central Park while she finished her work. Carol told Linda she would pick her up in three hours. She made a plan that Linda was to meet her at this specific bench at 8:00 PM. Linda agreed.

She began her walk. As it became dusk around 7:45, Linda started back to the bench where Carol planned to pick her up. However, she wasn't quite certain if she had found the correct bench. Linda preferred not to call her sister and bother her at work. So, she sat on the bench until darkness rolled in. She became a bit stressed. Wouldn't you know it, there happened to be a power grid outage in that area of New York and all the lights went out. No sky-line lights, no lights in Central Park! How scary?

A man sat down on the opposite end of the bench eight feet from Linda. They both sat there for a bit and he leaned toward her and asked, "Are you scared?" Her heart started to beat; her hands started to sweat. She quickly mumbled a bunch of her thoughts in a nervous response sharing the entire situation and how scared she really was at the moment.

He said, "Don't be scared. I walk this every day and I'll stay with you until your sister arrives." She felt a bit of relief.

After several moments of silence, she asked, "How can you be so calm?"

He said, "This is just an inconvenience - not a problem. The lights will come back on eventually and you will be safely home with your sister soon!"

She asked, "How can you think that way?"

He said," I was on the third floor of the World Trade Tower on 9-11 and I luckily escaped. That day was a problem - this situation tonight, just an inconvenience!"

We need to decipher inconveniences from problems because quite often our smaller inconveniences alter our attitude for lengthy periods of time unnecessarily. Realize there is a huge difference between a lump in your oatmeal, a lump in your throat and a lump in your breast. Change the way you look at things and the way you look at things begin to change. Decide to control your attitude or your negative attitude will control you! Live for the attitude you want by consciously making the choice daily. Attitude is the difference between an ordeal and an adventure.

I would like to share a few tips on how to choose your attitude and infect others with your positive attitude.
- Choose your attitude by consciously thinking about the attitude YOU want for the day.
- Choose to have fun at work.
- Intermittently but consciously throughout the day, ask yourself, "Is my attitude positively infectious right now?"
- Decide each day who you would like to positively "infect" with your attitude.

- Look at your job as an opportunity - a way of making a life, not simply a living.
- Work on a healthy sense of self-esteem. Realize your talents and appreciate them daily.
- Be an extrovert. Step out of your box and live.
- Be an optimist. Try looking for the good in all things, events and situations.
- Understand that everything you do may be a "once in a lifetime opportunity."
- Live with a plan that addresses all your bucket lists.
- Live in the moment more often.
- Sincerely love those you do love and let them know by your actions AND your words.
- Learn to differentiate a problem from an inconvenience.

We must begin practicing what I call *attitude paradigm shifts* while at work, with our families and in public. Given the following situations, what might you consider doing differently with a more positive attitude?

- A fellow employee, supervisor or boss makes a statement demoralizing you.
- There are members of a team you are on within your business "not pulling their load."
- Your boss or supervisor doesn't seem to trust you as a professional.
- Someone flips you off traveling down the road.
- You are very excited to get to your vacation destination and the airline has lost your luggage.
- You are returning home from a funeral of a colleague or relative who unexpectedly passed away.
- You've been waiting 45 minutes for a doctor's appointment and you are frustrated because your time is as valuable as well.

To conclude this chapter, I'd like to leave you with some quotes on your priceless attitude. They could be an integral part of your life's plan - your daily mission. Don't you love pilots that stand with a positive attitude and greet you and the hundreds of other passengers with direct eye contact and a genuine smile after they have safely landed? You can be that pilot. You can have that attitude daily *flying your plane*, living your life.

Here are a few quotes to consider:

- There are seven days in the week and *someday* isn't one of them. Begin today to choose your daily attitude.

- Your attitude determines your altitude.

- You cannot control what happens to you, but you can control your attitude in response to those things that do happen to you.

- A strong mental attitude may enhance the medication taken for mental health related conditions.

So, let's move to the next chapter with a renewed confidence with the ability to choose your attitude daily. Your positive attitude ought to affect your co-pilot, *your spouse, significant other, friend, colleague or an acquaintance.* Your positive attitude ought to infect your employees and *your passengers.* In essence, your positive attitude should affect your entire life. It will help you live with more passion, more intention and more purpose. Continue your *flight* with an attitude that everyone, including yourself, truly admires.

SAFE FLIGHT CHECKLIST:

- Start your day with an intentional choice of the attitude YOU want for the day.
- Realize your attitude is extremely powerful and can directly impact and affect the way you live.
- Choose to *infect* others in a very positive way with your attitude.
- Begin to utilize your attitude paradigm shifts in situations that normally deflate your positive attitude.

YOUR FLIGHT ACTION PLAN:

1. Write down instances, situations and behaviors that give you energy and directly affect your attitude.

2. In order to keep your mental and emotional energy high, discuss with someone the strategies you have decided to keep a more positive attitude.

3. For 24 hours, choose not to be negative at all. Try it! From the time you get up to the time you put your head on your pillow. If successful, try two days, etc.

   - Go to the companion website at **www.intentionallivinguniversity.com** for more articles, suggested books, video clips, etc.

Chapter 6

Setting Goals and Creating Bucket Lists
"Hope and anticipation attainment with
smooth-sailing and no regrets ahead"

As the pilot of your plane, do you have some goals in mind? Goals that will bring reassurance that the remaining portion of *your flight* is a good one – one with few regrets. Are some of these goals more important than others? Some, not so important? Every pilot, every passenger, every airline wants a safe flight. The mere anticipation of a safe flight is crucial. The hope from the pilot and the passengers that the flight will be safe is necessary. Just as an airplane's flight plan has goals, all of us in our lives need them. These goals may include a bucket list.

A bucket list is a written-out list of things that a person would like to do, achieve, experience, etc. before they "kick the bucket" or die. Notice, I mentioned that this bucket list should be in writing and posted where you can see it daily. A goal not written is simply a wish. Written goals have a way of transforming wishes into wants, cant's into cans, dreams into plans and plans into reality. Bucket lists can

include things to do, places to go, experiences you would like to have, a relationship with a higher
power, a faith focus, etc. Anyone who believes in God, a spirit or a higher power could certainly add these to their personal, spousal or family bucket lists.

John Dewey said, "Without some goals and some efforts, no man can live!" When we are motivated by goals that have deep meaning and we strive to complete them, then we REALLY LIVE! By both having them and writing them down, we acquire hope and anticipation. This leads us to take action.

If you, the pilot, didn't know the destination of your plane, you and everyone onboard would certainly be very concerned. If you don't know where you are going in your life, you simply might end up somewhere you never intended to be! Written goals and bucket lists are critical to your overall plan to live a self-directed flight.

Think about this statement for a moment. *You get what you "set out" to do*. If you don't intentionally set out to do the things you want, your outcome might possibly be regrets. Most of us have the sight but don't take the time for a vision that includes goals, bucket lists within a PLAN.

I challenge you to write your bucket list and display it where you will see it daily. The items on your list will act as daily reminders. They also act as motivators. I personally have my bucket lists displayed in my office along with a galvanized bucket to remind me daily of the little things I need to do to achieve my next goal. They give people HOPE and ANTICIPATION, two things we need especially when we are down and possibly depressed. After you have an enjoyable time writing your list, I suggest you share it with those you love, those who you care about or those who are interested in your life.

In addition to your own personal bucket list, I also would suggest that you take the opportunity and write the following bucket lists:

*Your spouse or significant other: Things you'd like to do together before one of you dies.

*A best friend: Things you'd like to do together before it's too late.

*Your children: Things you'd like to do with them before they enter high school, college, before they marry, by the end of the year, etc.

*Your grandchildren: Things you'd like to do with your grandchildren before they are 6, 12, 18 years of age.

*Your family: Things you'd like to accomplish together as a family before children begin going off to college, moving out or simply moving on in life.

As you may well be aware, I had the unbelievable honor of teaching for approximately 33 years. Most of those years I taught middle school health education. I would give my students the assignment of writing 15 things on their bucket list. The sky was the limit. I did set parameters. Those things on their bucket lists had to be healthy, legal and safe. They should be on yours as well. One student came the next day with 206 items on her list! Yes, 206 items and she was all excited. She thanked me for giving her that assignment and stated that she and her mother were immediately going to Walmart after school and were going to purchase a packet of brightly colored 4 x 6 cards. On each card she said, she was going to write down one of her goals - items from her long bucket list. She then said she would take each card, tie a piece of her dad's fishing string to it and hang each one of the 206 cards from her bedroom ceiling. As she accomplished each one, she shared that she would take it down and post it on her bedroom door. My immediate

---

thoughts were, "There's a girl that is going places! She has too many things to do rather than those things that are not healthy, not legal and not safe!" She was FULL of hope and anticipation. I sincerely hope she is enjoying her life based on her middle school list! You can too!

The hope and anticipation alone will be a benefit of these lists. Fulfilling items on the list is a huge bonus! Crossing all of them off the list after accomplishing or attaining them is absolutely enjoyable as well! I suggest if you do reach that point of acquiring all the items on any bucket list, you begin writing another. What a way to live! What a way to make dreams, wishes, goals and desires come to reality.

Bucket lists are usually listed as bulleted items on a list. If you write down some goals to ATTAIN those items on your bucket lists, I would like to suggest an effective way to write those goals. Make sure they are S.M.A.R.T. goals. The "S" can remind you that your action towards meeting that goal needs to be written with *specifics*. The "M" can remind you that the action needs to be *measurable*. The "A" reminds the goal setter that the behaviors need to be *attainable and action related*. The "R" reminds you that the action needs be *relevant and realistic*. The "T" reminds the goal setter that it ought to be *time-bound.*

For example, I might have a goal to lose weight. Is that a good goal? Maybe. Is it a smart, action-oriented goal? No. That goal might be written like this: I will attempt to lose 10 pounds in the next 60 days by eating less and working out (lifting weights, doing aerobics, swimming, etc.) for 1-2 hours at the club each week. This goal is specific, measurable, attainable and action-related, relevant and realistic and its time bound.

Writing out your specific goals for your items on your bucket list(s) is critical to success attainment. I enthusiastically challenge you to write your top three personal, friend or family goals that will begin to allow you to achieve the items on your bucket lists using the S.M.A.R.T. goal principle. I believe that the goals you will write and post will allow you to have more balance in your life, more hope, more anticipation, more energy, a more positive attitude and less stress.

Finding your direction in life and writing your goals related to that direction are essential. It may mean that you can actually live a longer life. According to Dan Buettner, author of *The Blue Zones Solution* (2012), a book I would highly recommend reading, "Researchers attribute longer lifespan to finding a direction in life and setting goals related to it."[2]

So, as you comfortably sit back in your pilot's seat with *autopilot* engaged, enjoy your remaining flight, the weather ahead and your safe landing. In your life, think about the years you have remaining, your final days and most importantly, what you want to accomplish before your final descent. Your goals and bucket lists will have a significant impact on how you will plan to live the rest of your life. Think about them, write them down, post them and begin attaining them. Life is short and you ought to go *full throttle ahead* and enjoy living the rest of your life.

SAFE FLIGHT CHECKLIST:

- Setting goals and writing bucket lists provides continual hope and anticipation.
- Writing and displaying your goals and bucket lists allow you to be reminded of them and attained more readily.
- Think about weaving your goals and bucket list into your life's mission statement, plan or vision.

YOUR FLIGHT ACTION PLAN:

1. Set aside some time in the next week or two to sit down and begin writing your own bucket list. If you have one, get it out, add to or delete from it and make it visible.

2. After you have written whatever bucket list you have chosen, pick your top one, two or three items and begin to write specific action steps. These steps increase the chances that this item will occur and be attained. Use the S.M.A.R.T. goal setting principle.

3. Share this bucket list and goal setting thought process with your children as early as possible so they will want to write their own, as well. The research is clear that children that have written down, attainable and specific goals and bucket lists are much happier, healthier and more successful. It is one of the heavily researched Developmental Assets concluded by the Search Institute.

   - Go to the companion website at **www.intentionallivinguniversity.com** for more articles, suggested books, video clips, etc.

Chapter 7

Change
"Small positive changes in your flight pattern predicate bigger changes ahead"

Just as a pilot follows a *flight plan,* primarily done via a computer, you are the pilot of your life with a plan purposely developed by you. This results in having more satisfaction, happiness and less regret.

Small changes now can have dramatic effects later in your life. Jon Rohn from his website, entitled, www.myowneulogy.com has stated, "Your life doesn't get better by chance, it gets better by change."[3]

Change is difficult, especially if you are a 30-year seasoned pilot or a 60-year-old person who has been set in your ways. Every change in your life will come down to starting or stopping something. I would like to ask that you do a quick assessment of your life and ask yourself, "What would I like to change in my life? What can I stop? What could I start?" If you have some ideas about change in your life, this chapter will give you the direction you may need to catapult that change. Usually, once small changes occur, people gain the confidence to make more continual and sustainable changes in their lives. Keep in mind, change comes easier with an open mind and a positive attitude. Realize change is an inevitable part of life.

To identify where you are as far as change-readiness, thirty-five years of research clearly exhibit specific stages of change. The research is called the Transtheoretical Model (TTM). (Prochaska and DiClemente, 1983, Prochaska, DiClemente and Norcross, 1992).[4] It uses *Five Stages of Change* to integrate the most powerful principles and processes of change. It was developed from leading theories of counseling and behavior change. It is based on principles developed from scientific research, intervention development and scores of empirical studies. I will paraphrase these five stages for you so that you can identify what stage you are in when considering any lifestyle changes you wish to make.

Precontemplation Stage - (Not Ready)

People in the Precontemplation Stage do not intend to take action in the foreseeable future, usually measured as the next six months. Being uninformed or under informed about the consequences of one's behavior may cause a person to be in the Precontemplation Stage. Multiple unsuccessful attempts at change can lead to demoralization about the ability to change. Pre-contemplators are often characterized as resistant, unmotivated or unready for help. The fact is, traditional programs for change were not ready for such individuals and were not designed to meet their needs.

I'll use smoking as just one example of change here. In this stage, the smoker isn't informed or doesn't want to be informed of the consequences so isn't going to quit at any time in their future.

Contemplation Stage - (Getting Ready)

The Contemplation Stage is when you intend to change within the next six months. They are more aware of the pros of changing, but are also acutely aware of the cons. In a meta-analysis across 48 health risk behaviors, the pros and cons of changing were equal (Hall & Rossi, 2008). This weighting between the costs and benefits of changing can produce profound ambivalence that can cause people to remain in this stage for long periods of time. This phenomenon is often characterized as chronic contemplation or behavioral procrastination. Individuals in the Contemplation Stage are not ready for traditional action-oriented programs that expect participants to act immediately.

Here, the smoker is starting to say, "I must quit by a certain date." They generally know the consequences of smoking on their body, but they are procrastinating – "one more day" – "I'll quit next month, etc."

Preparation Stage - (Ready)

The Preparation Stage is the stage in which you intend to take action in the immediate future, usually measured as the next month. Typically, they have already taken some significant action in the past year. These individuals have a plan of action, such as joining a gym, consulting a counselor, talking to their physician or relying on a self-change approach. These are the people who should be recruited for action-oriented programs.

The smoker now is ready. They are prepared mentally, physically and emotionally. They already have taken some actions to reduce the amount of smoking. They are right on that edge of commitment.

Action Stage

Action is the stage in which you have made specific overt modifications in their lifestyles within the past six months. But in the TTM, Action is only one of five stages. Typically, not all modifications of behavior count as Action in the Five Stages of Change model. In most applications, people must attain a criterion that scientist and professionals agree is sufficient to reduce risk of disease. For example, if someone is trying to improve their health by reducing the effects of nicotine, reducing the number of cigarettes or switching to low-tar and low nicotine cigarettes were considered acceptable actions. Now, the consensus is clear – only total abstinence counts. Presently, it is estimated that most people are in the following categories regarding change in their lives:

Precontemplation = 40%

Contemplation = 40%

Action = 20%

The smokers take specific actions to reduce or quit completely. They start to feel they have the control back and they feel proud.

The Maintenance Stage

Maintenance is the stage in which you have made specific overt modifications in their lifestyles and are working to prevent relapse; however, they do not need to apply change processes as frequently as do people in the Action Stage. While in the Maintenance Stage, people are less tempted to relapse and grow increasingly more confident that they can continue their changes. Based on self-efficacy data, researchers have estimated that the Maintenance Stage lasts from six months to about five years. While this estimate may seem somewhat pessimistic, longitudinal data in the 1990 Surgeon General's report support this temporal estimate. After 12 months of continuous abstinence, 43% of individuals returned to regular smoking. It was not until five years of continuous abstinence that the risk for relapse dropped to 7% (HHS).[5]

Here, the smoker gains pride by stating, "I haven't smoked a cigarette for this long and this is what I have done..." Confidence is overflowing and they continue to make their change a life-long and a sustainable one.

"Metathesiophobia" or the fear of change is a real concern here. I would like to suggest challenging your fears with a positive change list. Change can be extremely difficult for most. But when you intentionally think about the positives that can come from it, research clearly indicates that we can build a toughness, a willingness to continue a change through impending big or small changes. Sometimes, if we prepare ourselves for change, it lessens the potential difficulty of that change. Try making a list of all the positives that could come out of an impending change. When done, write another list of the many positive results that have come about from previous changes you have made. Taking preliminary actions on impending changes puts power in your hands and may remove some of the anxiety from attempting any changes in your future.

As you think of behaviors you'd like to change, you need to consider your past conditioning, your past programming – those previous positive or negative experiences that have set our brains to deal with change. As we are provided with positive experiences, our brain neurons begin to foster, develop and grow in our brain. The more neurons developed from positive and successful experiences, the more change and learning takes place. The more negative experiences we have encountered, the more difficult it is for our brains to make the changes we may desire. I know of a lot of people who "want" to change, but their pre-disposed conditioning makes it extremely difficult for them. To make changes stick and remain sustainable, one must make little changes, so that the brain can manufacture those needed neurons. Little by little, you will feel success. Once you've made one minor change, begin the process with another. As you consider change, I want you to know that there is a myriad of influences that literally program our brain's hardware. We simply must recognize that principle and begin to make small changes that eventually will lead to major change.

So, think of some of the changes you'd like to make in your life. Identify what stage you are in and plan your action or non-action accordingly. If you are struggling to think of possible changes you may want to entertain, here are just a few suggestions:

- Smoking (risk reduction or quitting)
- Healthy eating or dietary fat reduction or weight management
- Reducing risk factors for cardiovascular disease prevention
- Counseling
- Stress management
- Time management
- Adjusting your attitude
- Balancing your life – personally, professionally and with your family
- Adoption of physical activity
- Cervical cancer prevention
- Mammography screening
- Prevention of skin cancer
- Alcohol & drug use
- Preventive medicine behaviors
- Oral self-care-flossing
- Meditation - Yoga
- Mindful thinking
- Praying or deepening your spiritual life
- Reduction of salt and sugar in-take
- Reduction of diet soda or "pop" for you Midwesterners
- Managing your stress
- Recycling
- Being more positive
- Communicating more effectively
- Becoming more romantic or loving
- Having more fun in life

- Worrying Less – wishing or praying more
- Saving money more efficiently
- Changing jobs
- Sharing feelings more often
- Anger management
- Retiring
- Getting married or divorced

Here are a few thoughts about change to read over, think about and then consider when you contemplate any changes in your life.

- Change always seems difficult, but research clearly demonstrates it eventually makes us stronger.
- One reason people resist change is because they focus on what they have to give up instead of what they have to gain.
- Change is hard at first, messy in the middle and satisfying at the end.
- If you want change, you have to be willing to be uncomfortable.
- Great things never came from comfort zones.
- Sometimes change can be scary. If the positive change scares you, it might be something you want to try.
- Change may come from fear. Embrace it.
- Sometimes change is not only good for you but everyone else around you as well.
- Socrates said, *"The secret of change is to focus all of your energy, not on fighting the old, but building the new."*
- You can't start on the new chapter of your life if you keep re-reading the last one.
- If you want something you've never had, do something you've never done.

- You will never change your life unless you change something you do daily.
- The secret of change is found in your daily routine.
- Life has no remote. You have to get up and change it yourself.

According to Steve Mariboli from his website www.stevemariboli.com, "Incredible change happens in your life when you decide to take control of what you do have power over instead of craving control of what you don't."6 According to a website titled, www.perfectharmony.com, "Changing behavior is like driving down an old, rutted, dirt road." In order to get out of the rut and onto to a new path, you need to jerk the steering wheel hard. If you don't jerk the wheel hard enough, you'll just bounce back in the same old rutted path again. So, for change to happen, hold on tight, jerk the wheel as hard as you can and get ready for a bumpy ride. Change is just beyond, on the other side. A website, www.lovethatpic.com shares this quote regarding change. "Making a big life change is pretty scary. But, know what's even scarier? Regret." Sometimes change occurs when we're tired of certain aspects in our life making us become complacent.

Yet another website, www.viacuriano.com shares a profound statement regarding change. *The 3 C's in Life: Choice, Chance and Change. You must make the Choice to take the Chance if you want anything to Change in your life.*

David Winograd, a proofreader for my book, wrote the following poem that provides a "tongue in cheek" thought to why some people just can't change because it's everyone else's fault setting them up in the lifestyle they are in presently. A few of his other poems will be shared in other chapters as well. It goes like this:

An Honest Evaluation

I'm creating a list
And there's a lot on my mind
The behaviors to adopt
Those I should leave behind

But I'm having a problem
And my list is quite small
In fact, at this time
I have nothing at all

See I have no problems
I have nothing to say
It's the other-the system
That leads me astray

It's so very evident
And everyone can see
That there's absolutely nothing
At all wrong with me

This thought process is believed by many. We all have issues, baggage and problems that seep into our lives. Often, they make us believe things CANNOT change. We all need to understand it is you that can acquire the knowledge, power and skills to make any necessary personal changes.

So, there's still time to change. As you *pilot* your life, you can still make necessary changes as you fly through the many *wind shears and storms* of life. Know that you can change the course of your flight at any time, if you are mindful and deliberate in your actions. Determine what TTM Stage you're in on your *flight.* Then with passion, purpose and intention, choose some bigger, more challenging changes that will predicate directing the way your plane flies, *the way you live.* Start small and make those little subtle changes. Go ahead, sit comfortably in your cockpit and begin to make some changes today that will direct your *flight, destination and your landing.*

Pilots often say, "'A small correction over time adds up." It is the same with change. Make your small corrections, your changes that will steer you in the direction YOU want to go in your life. Continual smaller corrections can lead to major destination changes.

SAFE FLIGHT CHECKLIST:

- When making changes, try to make changes that are sustainable
- Realize you most likely will be uncomfortable with any change
- When considering change, determine what stage of change you are in and make the necessary plans accordingly- precontemplation, contemplation, preparation, action and maintenance
- Change should be thought about and written in your life's mission/vision/plan

YOUR FLIGHT ACTION PLAN:

1. Today, create a POSITIVE CHANGE LIST and change your mindset from some impending shake-up or change.

2. Write down what you would like to change, then list all the positive things that could come from it.

3. Discuss those things that might hamper each desired change with someone significant in your life.

4. Act! Choose one small change that you have listed and work on it for 14 days until it becomes a habit.

    - Go to the companion website at **www.intentionallivinguniversity.com** for more articles, suggested books, video clips, etc.

Chapter 8

Priority Management:
Spending your Time Wisely
*"Intentionally planning to fly happier world-wide
with more satisfaction based on your priorities"*

Time. There never seems to be enough of it. It often stresses us out. It quite often goes by quickly. It happens. It is limited. Time is irreversible. Time is irreplaceable. Time is life. To waste your time is to waste your life. To master your life, you need to master your time. Time ticks twenty-four hours a day, seven days a week and continues without ever stopping. As you well know, when flying, all flights are timed from departure to arrival. When living, our lives are *timed* from arrival to departure. "Had a great flight" is a common response after your flight arrives on time without turbulence. My wish for you is *to have a great life* according to YOUR plan so that you can live fully and then *land* with few regrets. **If you don't take some time to PLAN the life you want, you will eventually be forced to spend a lot of time dealing with a life you did not want!** Our twenty-four-hour days are like suitcases. Some people can get more into them. Why? They PLAN and make things fit. They prioritize what they really need in their suitcases and make those things fit, sometimes by rolling the clothes, putting them in airtight bags or eliminating items they can get along without. So, as the pilot of your life, I suggest that you seriously look at your priorities and how you *spend* your time. Yes, how you *spend* it. It is priceless. Spending it wisely is critical!

Think about the time you have left like a bank account. Imagine there is a bank account that credits your account each morning with $86,400. It carries over no balance from day to day. Every evening the account deletes whatever part of the balance you failed to use that day. What would you do? Draw out every cent, right? Each of us have such a bank account. It's called TIME. Every morning it credits you with 86,400 seconds. Every night, it deletes the time you have failed to use or have not invested in a good purpose. It carries over no balance. It allows no overdraft. Each day, it opens a new account for you. Each night, it burns the remains of the day. If you fail to use the day's deposits, the loss is yours and it cannot ever be regained. There is no going back to check the registry for irregularities and imbalances. There also is no drawing against tomorrow. You really need to live in the present on today's deposits. Invest it wisely so you can get the most out of your health and happiness. The clock is running. Make the most of every day. Treasure and appreciate the moments more often. Time waits for no one. Yesterday is history. Tomorrow is a mystery. Today is a gift. That's why they call today the present! Use your daily bank deposit wisely with intention and purpose. This can be achieved by planning your day, week, months and life. Just as there is fuel put in the airplane you are flying, there is time given to use each day; like fuel, it eventually does run out.

We seem to have more time-saving devices than ever before such as computers, microwaves, phones with instant information acquisition (Alexa, Siri), fast food, faster transportation, etc. Yet, we all commonly share the realization, "There never seems to be enough time." Steven Covey, in his book, *Seven Habits of Highly Effective People*, shared that *Americans are the most time-deprived people in the world. They have convinced themselves that despite all of the high-tech time-saving devices at their disposal, they are doomed to terminal "busy-ness."* As Americans we are the number one country

—
92

in the world for taking the least amount of vacation time. I believe that if we never seem to have enough time, we simply want too much. If your needs are many and it takes too much time to acquire or maintain them, then you want too much. Think about that statement as you develop your plan to live for your priorities. Focusing on your life's priorities and begin spending time on them with passion and intention. This is what fundamental time management is all about. Successful people don't find time, they make it. Again, it's about what your priorities are and how you intentionally focus your time on those priorities that are important to you and your life. If you really think about it, no one is busy in this world; it's really all about their priorities. So, what are your top five priorities in life? Think about them now. If you need to, write them down. Steven Covey, also in his book, shares that one of his researched seven habits is to "put first things first." In other words, focus on your priorities in life. So, save the excuses. It's not about having the time. It's about making the time. If it matters, you will make the time. Period!

There is a story about managing your time that should force you to think of your priorities. It's written by an unknown author.

Dust If You Must

A house becomes a home when you can write "I love you" on the coffee table.

I can't believe all the time I spend CLEANING! I used to spend six to eight hours every weekend making sure our home was clean and that everything was perfect - just in case someone might come over. Then I realized that no one ever came over! They were all out living their lives and spending time on their priorities. Now, with my different perspective on how I spend my time, I find no need to explain the "condition" of my home. They are there to hear about everything I have been doing - living! If you haven't figured this out yet, heed this advice. Life is short. Enjoy it. Live it. Appreciate it. Slow down. Dust if you must, but wouldn't it be better to plan and focus on living, to have fun and to create memories? Dust if you must, but the world is out there. Today will never come around again. Dust if you must but bear in mind that eventually old age will come, and it may not be so kind. And when you go......and go we all must.... you, yourself will make more dust! So, dust if you must or live your priorities.

I would like to share five keys to mastering your time that may assist you when writing your life's mission statement or life's plan.

- Plan your day and base it on your priorities. Utilize the TO DO List we shared with you earlier in the book. Plan for balance personally, professionally and with your family while focusing on your priorities.
- Make appointments with yourself! You are more apt to keep those appointments. Taking care of yourself first is critical to your overall time management.
- Use the little bit-at-a-time approach. Do a little bit on those bigger projects by slotting in a specific amount of time each day towards completion of that project that may be hanging over your head.
- Know your most productive time and do your most important work during that time. Morning? Day? Night-time?
- Slow down and appreciate the moments that you experience during your day.

Many people think they are busy, but they are actually wasting time. I would like to suggest you consider the following fifteen ways to quit wasting your time.

- Figure out your goals-your priorities and begin to focus on balancing your personal, professional and family life.

- Keep track how long it takes you to do things. Knowing how you plan to "spend it" allows for more efficient time management.
- Prioritize your TO DO's into four groups—1) Urgent 2) Not urgent, but important 3) Urgent, but not important 4) Neither urgent or important.
- Schedule your day with my recommended daily TO DO List.
- Don't cheat on your daily planned TO DO List.
- Write down all the things you need to do.
- Do the hard stuff first.
- Decide if the task at hand is worth your time.
- Just start it - find ways to push through without putting it off.
- Realize all time counts - even a 15-minute spurt.
- Use your computer and technology to assist in the saving of time whenever possible.
- Set time limits on your tasks.
- Realize that e-mailing, texting, being on Facebook or Instagram, internet shopping can quickly add up to a "black-hole of time."
- Take time to eat lunch or snack so you are energized enough to do the rest of your TO DO List.
- Schedule and plan activities for yourself, your spouse and your family.

Time does have a way of showing us what really matters. Just ask someone on their deathbed. Buddha once said, "The trouble is, you think you have time." Begin to learn to appreciate what you have before time makes you appreciate what you had! A psychologist named David L. Weatherford wrote a poem from the perspective of a terminally ill 13-year-old girl. In this poem the girl states, *Slow down, don't dance so fast, time is short, the music won't last. When you run so fast to get somewhere, you miss half the fun of getting there. Life is not a race. Do take it slower. Hear the music before the song is over.*

In this poem, this 13-year-old girl who is terminally ill eloquently states the importance of time.

Appreciating the time, one has *spent* is critical even after death. Have you gone to a cemetery and looked at the gravestones? I mean really looked at the gravestones. You may see a name, a date of birth, a date of death and possibly a Bible verse or a quote. But what we often don't see is the dash between the birth and death on the headstone. I would like to share this poem, written by Linda Ellis, www.linda-ellis.com, titled, *The Dash*.[7]

I read of a man who stood to speak
At the funeral of a friend
He referred to her tombstone
From the beginning to the end.

He noted that first came her date of birth
And spoke the following date with tears,
But he said what mattered most of all
Was the dash between those years.

For that dash represents all the time
That she spent alive on earth
And now only those who loved her
Know what that little line was worth.

For it matters not, how much we own,
The cars, the house, the cash
What matters is how we live and love
And how we spend our dash.

So, think about this long and hard
Are there things you'd like to change?
For you never know how much time is left,
That still can be rearranged.

——

If we could just slow down enough
To consider what's true and real,
And always try to understand
The way all other people feel.

And be less quick to anger
And show appreciation more
And love the people in our lives
Like we have never loved before.

It we treat each other with respect,
And more often wear a smile
Remembering that this special dash
May last a short, short while.

So, when your eulogy is being read
With your life's actions to rehash
Would you be proud of the things they say?
Or about how you spent your dash?

How are you spending your dash? Are you happy with your *expenditures*? As the pilot of your *flight,* how do you want to spend the rest of your life? Seriously stop and think about that and remember to include this in your final life's plan at the end of the book. To help you determine what you like or dislike about how you normally spend your day, your time, make a circle on a sheet of paper, title it, "My Normal Day" and divide it into four 6-hour quadrants. Imagine it as a normal day. Section off approximately how much time you do the following on a normal day in your life. Estimate minutes by dividing the number of hours in the week you do that activity. Write the amount of time spent on each of the topics listed below on your circle.

- Sleeping
- Working

- Personal Care (showering, dressing, preparing body for the day) - AM and PM
- Personal leisure time (exercising, gardening, walking, reading, etc.)
- Eating, cooking, and cleaning up after three meals
- Travel time
- Quality family time
- Time with friends - socially
- Quality time with spouse
- Housekeeping (washing clothes, ironing, folding clothes, cleaning, bed-making, bill paying, lawn mowing, watering plants, shoveling, etc.)
- Social media time (TV, computer, e-mailing, texting and video games)
- Spiritual and reflection time (praying and reflecting)
- Relaxation time

When done, play the song, "Live Like you are Dying" by Tim McGraw and begin to write down things you like and things you don't like about what you see on your "Normal Day" sheet. Use this list for your eventual life's plan that you will write when you've completed this book. You'll readily see where you are *spending* your time. This will allow you to critically look at your priorities and decide whether or not you need to adjust the time you spend in each area.

So, you have another 24 hours. Hopefully, tomorrow and each day forward, you will have another day. Look at it as a new day, a gift. Use it as you will. You can waste it or use it for something good. You can go through the motions or look for moments with your priorities. What you do today, tomorrow and the next day are extremely important as you will be exchanging a day of your life for it! Take the time... for time! Life is short and we are dead for a whole lot longer than we are alive!

SAFE FLIGHT CHECKLIST:

- True time management is primarily based on your priorities.
- Identify ways we waste our time and focus on avoiding that behavior as much as possible.
- To value time, live like you may be dying.
- Realize that LOVE to our children is spelled TIME.

YOUR FLIGHT ACTION PLAN:

1. Share your normal day activity on how you spend your time with someone of significance and state some actions you may intend to change.

2. Make a list of how you could save more time for your priorities every day.

3. Begin to write on your TO DO List more time for you and then for your priorities. Remember, YOU should be your number one priority!

    - Go to the companion website at **www.intentionallivinguniversity.com** for more articles, suggested books, video clips, etc.

Chapter 9

Happiness: The Secret Ingredients
"You'll be surprised where it's stored on your plane"

"Don't worry, be happy..." We have all heard this saying or have listened to the song. As you pilot the remaining portion of your life, you can fly with more happiness and maintain that level of happiness only if you are satisfied with your focused plan or begin to develop your plan.

What would make you happier? A new house? A new relationship? A flatter stomach? More money? We should all understand that these things may make life easier or a bit nicer. But do they really give you happiness? Let's take a look at what the research says about happiness. Did you know that happy people generally don't give happiness much thought? The pursuit of happiness can actually backfire say experts at the University of Denver. People who place a real high value on happiness have, on average, 17 more symptoms of depression than those who don't. Lesson: don't search, don't crave, don't expect more happiness. Realize happiness is really within us. Researchers also say that American vacation-goers feel happiest when not on their vacation, but when they are planning it! Dutch researchers say they get elated from just the anticipation. Those researchers found that planning a vacation can improve your mood for up to two months before their actual trip. Unfortunately, the researchers also found, the moment the vacationers return home, they are no more content than someone who had gone away. Researchers have further concluded that 50% of our happiness is genetic, 10% comes from life experiences and the remaining 40% comes from how YOU think and act every day. This is key. We have control of almost half of our happiness!

There are numerous ways in which we can control our happiness. A Gallup poll found that the biggest determinant of job satisfaction and contentment was having a best-friend at the office. Dan Buettner, author of *Thrive: Finding Happiness the Blue Zones Way*, suggested getting to know your colleagues outside of work by organizing "social happy hours" or playing on a sports team with them.[8] According to researchers at the University of Maryland, people who read more often are happier than those who watch television even if their plot in the book is depressing! In a University of Rochester study, 90% of subjects got a boost in energy and their brightened their outlook by spending time outdoors around trees, grass and living creatures. And just because you see the glass half empty, doesn't mean you can't be happy. In fact, research has concluded that expecting the worst can actually make you less prone to depression, particularly during difficult events such as illness, a divorce or the death of a loved one. Lowered expectations mean less disappointments in life. Many studies have found that listening to music can also lift your spirits and any genre will work as long as it's music you enjoy. Elizabeth Lombardo, in her book, *A Happy You: Your Ultimate Prescription for Happiness,* stated that for some it's Bach and for some it's heavy metal.[9]

Studies have also found that a daily fish oil supplement can be as effective as prescription drugs in treating depression. Terese Aubele, coauthor of a book: *Train your Brain to be Happy*, says fish oil rich in Omega 3 fatty acids increase your brain's ability to receive mood-boosting signals from the "feel-good" hormones like serotonin and norepinephrine.[10] And, just imagining yourself laughing can reduce sadness. According to research from Nakia Gordon at Bowling Green University. "We scanned subjects' brains and found that the areas that indicate happiness lit up whether subjects were actually laughing or simply thinking about it."[11] And the research goes on. But there are a few components of "finding your happiness" that may surprise you. The remaining portion of this chapter will clarify those "secret ingredients."

Happiness really is a choice, as well as an internal search. Happiness is received when one focuses on what is internal that makes you happy such as your passions and priorities! Groucho Marx said, "Each morning I open my eyes and say to myself: I, not events or material things, have the power to make me happy today." This is vital to understand. Happiness is not determined by what is around you but rather what is happening inside you. Most people depend on others to gain happiness, but the true happiness comes from within. If you want to be happy - BE! How? Look within yourself and identify your passions, your priorities, the life events and experiences that make you happy. Begin to plan your day around them if possible. Quite often, it's about finding peace, joy, your spirit and calmness in your life: those priceless commodities that really matter such as love, your spouse, your family, etc. Think about quality commodities not the quantity of them!

Remember, happiness in your life is 40% within your control. For the most part, these things you can control outweigh the life circumstances and the genes you have that are out of your control. Below is a short list of possible things that can be controlled by you that have a direct impact on your own happiness.

- Living with a purpose - which is the main purpose of this book, writing out your life's vision plan and living it daily.
- Cultivating a thought process of optimism.
- Nurturing relationships.
- Doing activities that truly engage you.

- Practicing kindness.
- Being grateful.
- Counting your blessings.
- Learning to forgive.
- Practicing spirituality, your faith and taking actions based on your beliefs.
- Developing healthy coping strategies.
- Acting on your passions.

If you choose to find the positive in virtually every situation, you will be blessed. If you choose to find the negative, you will be commonly angry. As with happiness, this is largely YOUR decision to make!

Marci Shimoff and Carol Kline, authors of the book, *Happy for No Reason,* have shared some secrets of true happiness. They interviewed over 100 people whose happiness was not based on external circumstances. The people they studied were happy for no reason because they brought their happiness TO their experiences rather than trying to extract happiness FROM them.[12] These are the five keys they concluded from their study:

- **DON'T BELIEVE EVERYTHING YOU THINK!**

    We normally have about 50,000 conscious thoughts daily and if you swarm your brain with the negative thoughts, it can have a PROFOUND physiological effect! If you get ten compliments and one criticism, what do you normally keep thinking about?

- **NOTICE THE THINGS THAT MAKE YOU HAPPY EVEN THOUGH THEY MAY BE VERY SMALL**

- **CHOOSE THE HAPPIER THOUGHT**

    Begin changing the way you think about your thoughts and choose to think about the positive ones.

- **TEND TO YOUR RELATIONSHIPS**

Strong relationships, male or female are one of the strongest predictors of happiness. Your relationships with women are even more important than those relationships with men. This is possibly due to the nature of women being better communicators and more open with their feelings. Appreciate all of your relationships and be thankful for them.

- **FIND PASSION AND PURPOSE**

Bring a sense of purpose to EVERY activity you do. Bring a sense of passion to mundane activities.

Gratitude is also a powerful process for shifting your energy and bringing more of what you want into your life. Be grateful for what you already have, and you will begin to attract more good things. Tell the people in your life that you are grateful for them or what they do in a truly genuine way. Being grateful for what you have and where you are today while thinking about your life as a gift opens the door for happiness. Appreciating every single day as a priceless gift is a very good start.

Happiness comes when we stop complaining about the troubles we have and offer thanks for all the troubles we don't have. Begin to let go of what is gone, be grateful for what remains and look forward to what is coming. Don't just hope, wish or dream for happiness. Look for happiness within while being thankful. If you pin your hopes, dreams and wishes on the future, you'll miss your chance at happiness. There is a huge difference of planning for your future with happiness in it and living in it. Find happiness within yourself *on your flight* and really begin enjoying your ride, again with passion and intention. Happiness is within us. If you pursue happiness, it will elude you. Happiness is like a butterfly. If you focus on your family, your friends, the needs of others, your work, your faith while trying the very best you can, happiness will find you! The more you chase it, the more it eludes you. Turn your attention to other things and it will come and sit gently on your shoulder.

There are FIVE TRAPS that ensnare people who are TRYING too hard to be happy:

- **Trying to Buy Happiness**

  Happiness really depends on your <u>expectations.</u>
  People find their happiness from within. Their status symbols are a happy family, good friends and pride in their work. Most millionaires have sacrificed freedom and/or leisure to become rich.

- **Continual Pleasure**

  Happy people know that it's wise to back away from life's banquet, so that pleasure will stay novel and refreshing. Too much of a good thing, being unhappy or sad are facts of life. Problems should be utilized. If you've never been unhappy, how would you know what being happy really is?

- **Not Resolving the Past**

  Some wounds may NEVER totally heal. Sometimes these wounds can become one's greatest motivators. Dwelling on them often can affect your daily attitude.

- **Not Overcoming Your Weaknesses**

  People change their lives every day. The focus is not to act on weaknesses, such as being a workaholic, but rather the focus is to act on strengths. Focusing on your strengths will reduce the power of your weaknesses.

- **Trying to Force Happiness**

Faking one's happiness is a real effort. It's debilitating. Just look within - your happiness is there already. You have EVERYTHING you need to BE happy in your life RIGHT NOW. Reflect and truly think about it regularly. It is an inside job. Don't assign anyone else that much power over your life!

Sometimes we work so hard for happiness. Simple suggestions include looking at the positive more frequently and worrying less. About 90% of the things that happen to us are good and only 10% are not. To be HAPPY, we must focus on the 90%. Try not to worry. Yesterday is gone. Tomorrow hasn't arrived yet. You have just one day - TODAY- be HAPPY IN IT.

If you are not sure what brings you happiness ask, "What is my joy/happiness?" As you commit to whatever that is, you will attract an avalanche of joyful and happy experiences because you're thinking and reflecting about the things that make you joyful and happy!

According to several professional development researchers, there are 12 things happy people do differently than unhappy people:

- They talk their way to happiness. They talk optimistically. For example, "I'm challenged right now vs. I'm overwhelmed right now."

- They exercise. People who exercise are generally happier and more upbeat! More exercise equates to more endorphins.

- They don't bury their emotions. They talk to a friend, write in a diary or paint their feelings or go in a soundproof room and just scream for 10 seconds

- They pamper themselves. They relax, treat themselves, reflect and do things that make them happy.

- They listen to HAPPY music. Usually music one grew up with equates to happier memories and feelings.

- They have a vision or purpose every day. They think of an interest, dream, goal, wish or a desire that allows them to get up and "make-it" through their day.

- They find happiness within themselves by intentionally focusing on their passions and they stop looking to others to supply their happiness.

- They take new risks that will make them happy. They may try a new class, a new skill without pressures to succeed.

- They keep the faith. They keep the anticipation. Whether it's spiritual or just believing something good will happen, increases the chance to be happy.

- They spend time with others. They develop strong relationships.

- They set goals including having a bucket list. ANTICIPATION simply makes one happy.

- They continue to PLAY! They never grow up.

So, take too many pictures, laugh too often and love like you've never been hurt. Every 60 seconds you spend upset is a minute of happiness you'll NEVER get back. My sincere wish for you is to return to the joy and happiness you may have experienced as a child. As you *pilot* the rest of your life, search within for those priorities, those things that make you happy and then begin to live for them. They may be a bit *covered up* and deep within the *storage area of your plane.* I suggest you continue to search until you find them. They will certainly help you live out your mission, your *flight* with grace, dignity and certainly happiness.

DON'T WORRY – BE HAPPY!

SAFE FLIGHT CHECKLIST:

- WE control our happiness.
- Happiness is an internal search and then a choice.
- There are things that happy people do differently.
- Just thinking happy thoughts will make one happier.

YOUR FLIGHT ACTION PLAN:

1. Make a list of those things in your life that make you happy. After each, brainstorm things that may be preventing you from that source of happiness. Use that list when writing your life's mission or vision statement.

2. If you are already happy, list the things you can do to maintain that happiness. If not, start by talking to someone you trust and share with them your personal quest to become happier.

3. Starting today, when making out your TO DO List, intentionally and consciously think about planning at least one to two events that will make you happy in that day!

   - Go to the companion website at **www.intentionallivinguniversity.com** for more articles, suggested books, video clips, etc.

Chapter 10

Humor and Laughter:
Medicine for the Funny Bone
"Criers, bladder-leakers, side ache-getters, UNITE - let's have a flight filled with laughter and make it an enjoyable and memorable one"

As you continue your flight, it is critical to understand the importance of humor and laughter. If you have flown, you know it's extremely comforting when the pilot, flight attendant or another passenger brings out a smile in you or makes you chuckle or laugh. It relaxes us, bonds us and it actually builds relationships. Laughing allows our brains to release endorphins and serotonin, which are the feel-good chemicals that give us "natural highs." Just think for a moment of how you feel after experiencing a good hearty laugh. Remember the last time you laughed so hard that you cried or possibly lost bladder control? I'm sure that positive memory still sticks - it was a good memory - something you'll never forget and never regret. Those moments that you create account for a smoother flight and a much happier way to live. As you plan the rest of your life, it is imperative to have the ability to laugh at yourself, as well as to laugh with others.

Remember Willard Scott's interview with that 103-year-old lady from Tennessee that I shared in a previous chapter? He asked her what her top three reasons were for living such a long life. Again, she immediately responded by saying number one was attitude! You have to have a positive attitude. He asked what the second reason was for her longevity. She immediately responded by saying olive oil. Yes, olive oil on most everything. After a pause, he asked what the third reason was for her 103 years of age. She instantly responded, "Jack Daniels and lots of it." After he controlled himself and they both laughed, she said, actually I don't drink, but it is important to laugh every day!

Laughter is one of the five keys to personal rejuvenation. Studying several professional development researchers, I have concluded there are five keys to your overall personal rejuvenation:

- Your ability to deal with wounds you may have while celebrating your gifts. Whether it be an abusive situation in your past, a death, a divorce, etc., one needs to positively deal with their wound(s) and let go while focusing on their talents and gifts bestowed upon them.
- Your ability to manage your time for your priorities and live a more balanced life.
- To intentionally choose the attitude you want for your present day ahead and every day.
- Look at your job as an opportunity. Make sure you are not just making a living but making a life by thoroughly enjoying what you do. Your job should be balanced within your life.
- Laugh daily. Actually, an average of 6.5 minutes of laughter every day is recommended.

Intentionally looking for opportunities to laugh will make your days, your life and your flight operate much more smoothly. The many benefits of laughter include no co-pay and are actually all free and easily attained. It has been stated that laughter is the medicine of life. After becoming aware and learning all of the health benefits of laughter, I believe we will have doctors writing prescriptions to have you "laugh more" by intention and on purpose. Yes, a prescription to laugh more, while acquiring the many health benefits directly related to this great activity. As a former teacher, I learned a very important lesson regarding learning and laughing. When you laugh, research says that more blood flow goes to the frontal lobe of your brain making whatever is taught to you immediately afterwards stay in your brain for a very significant period of time and maybe forever. Most class periods, I would start off with an appropriate joke, funny story or embarrassing moment. I believe information retention was a direct outcome of laughter beforehand.

Below are the physical, mental, emotional and social benefits to laughter. This list is shared so you can begin the realization of how important laughter actually is to your health and to your life.

- Improves circulation and allows more oxygen into your body so you feel better.
- Gives off enzymes to protect your stomach and intestines from ulcers.
- Reduces blood pressure and heart rate.
- Body gives off endorphins acting as a mild pain reliever.
- Helps the body fight infection.
- Gives your internal organs a workout.
- Increases antibody production in your saliva making you sick less often.
- Relaxes muscles and reduces stress hormones.
- Stabilizes your mood and decreases anxiety.
- Enhances communication with others and actually inspires creativity.
- Boosts immunity and gets rid of toxins with your tear secretion.
- Helps transport nutrients and oxygen to body tissues.
- Helps boost morale while it exercises your heart muscle.
- It's extremely healthy and not only allows you to live longer BUT have MUCH MORE FUN along the way.

Today, humor and laughter are needed more than ever in our lives. When stressed, frustrated, apathetic or angry, that's when we NEED to laugh! I believe that when the going gets tough, the tough start laughing! In a recent Harris poll, 67% of people interviewed stated humor was critical in a good relationship. I also believe that all five senses are incomplete without the sixth sense - the sense of humor! Think of those special people around you who make you laugh regularly. I would surmise that you have a good relationship with them. To succeed in life, you need three things: a wishbone, a backbone and a funny bone! As you know, laughing can also be contagious so start the "infection."

Speaking of your flight, your life's plan and integrating humor and laughter, I would like to share the following story. A Southwest Airlines flight attendant got on the intercom of a flight that had just taken off. She stated, "We have a passenger who is celebrating his ninety-ninth birthday today and this is his first flight ever!" Everyone cheered, everyone clapped and started to sing Happy Birthday. She then said, "And you can congratulate him on the way out because HE'S FLYING THE PLANE!"

The most wasted day is one where you have NOT laughed. I challenge you to surround yourself with people that make you laugh. Force yourself to look for situations that'll make you laugh. We all need and could use more laughter in our lives. Remember, growing old is mandatory - growing up is optional! After all, it certainly makes our trip or journey a more enjoyable one, more memorable and definitely a healthier one.

SAFE FLIGHT CHECKLIST:

- We all need to try and laugh an average of 6.5 minutes per day.
- Laughter is good medicine and there is no co-pay.
- There are many physical, mental, emotional and social benefits to laughter.
- We need humor and laughter the most when we are stressed, angry or sad.

YOUR FLIGHT ACTION PLAN:

1. Start today to look for ways to infuse more humor and laughter into your life.

2. Begin to laugh at yourself more often - don't take yourself so seriously.

3. Choose to be positively "infectious" with your humor.

4. Laugh more often, by intention, starting today - even if you lose bladder control. Forget about the reminder your mom would give you when going somewhere, "Make sure you have clean underwear on in case you get in an accident and have to be hospitalized!"

   - Go to the companion website at **www.intentionallivinguniversity.com** for more articles, suggested books, video clips, etc.

Chapter 11

Managing the Stressors in your Life
"Clearing the static from the attic and enjoying a relaxing flight"

Try and recollect the first time you ever flew on an airplane. It may have been a very anxious and stressful time. How many different ways did stress exhibit itself during that first flight? For me, it was heavy breathing, white knuckles, a feeling of loss of control, sweating and tightened muscles. Thoughts of traveling about 600 miles an hour *in the air* was cemented in my brain. After three or four flights, those physical, mental and emotional stressors became non-existent. Why? I learned to adapt and cope. I learned to look for the stress indicators. I learned to trust more and worry less. I learned to allow my mind to go elsewhere during the take-off and landing. This chapter will help you with your overall life's plan by learning how to efficiently and effectively deal with the stressors in your life. With your stressors under control, or at least in perspective, *your flight,* the rest of your life can be as relaxing as you desire. The sub-title of this chapter is, "Clearing the static from the attic and enjoying a relaxing flight." Practicing specific strategies to clear your mind, "the attic" will be addressed so that you can manage stress more efficiently and effectively. *Enjoying a relaxing flight* will address specific strategies to deflate stress and result in stress prevention. The title of this chapter encapsulates it all. The chapter is about the perception and management of your stressors: those things, events or people that cause you stress.

This significantly important chapter will provide a variety of practical strategies to keep in your *carry-on bag.* You know those items you may need immediate access to while in flight. As you enter a plane, you may check out the pilot and make mental judgements. As you locate your seat on the plane, you take in its actual location and the person(s) sitting next to and near you. Internalizing all of this information may cause stress directly due to your *perception.* So first and most importantly, you have to understand that you are the one most responsible for the stress in your life. Not from your spouse, your children, your colleagues, your neighbors or people you have to deal with while at work.

So, YOU are the primary person responsible for the amount of stress in your life. YOU allow all of your stress to affect you. Understanding this, it is critical that you have an intentional and purposeful plan to deal with those things that cause you stress before they pile up. Are you aware that ninety percent of your stress is perceptual? Again, it is how you perceive your stressors that make you distressed. I have always liked this quote written by an anonymous writer. "It doesn't matter if your glass is half full or half empty; it's that it is refillable."
Stress is really about your perception and your attitude towards those people and events that naturally appear and occur around you. The key to managing stress lies within YOUR mind and heart.

So, as you observe the *flashing warning light on the dashboard - relaxation flight interrupter,* be ALARMED! It is STRESS! Stress can be unhealthy, yet at times beneficial. Stress can be defined in several ways. Stress is the innate response that allows us to respond to the physical, mental, social and emotional demands of life. Stress is also an ignorant state. Consistent stressors often do

make people believe that everything is an emergency. Stress can be caused by attempting to have power over things that are beyond one's control. Stress can
also be caused by how we emotionally respond to what happens to us. Stress is not *what* happens to us. It is our *response* to what happens. THIS RESPONSE IS A CHOICE!

As you may know, stress is linked to the top six leading causes of death: heart disease, cancer, lung ailments, accidents, cirrhosis of the liver and suicide. If you truly want to *enjoy your ride - your flight,* it is necessary to deal with your stress with a pre-thought-out plan. First, it is necessary to identify the factors that increase your chances of stress exhaustion.

They include:

- Negative perception – the worry-wart syndrome.
- Family pressures.
- Work problems.
- Negative coping strategies.
- Responsibility without gratitude.
- Lack of coping skills.
- Broken compass - no purpose or plan to live.
- Personal tragedy.
- Helper mentality.

Once identified, you have taken a major first step. Determining the factors that cause you stress is critical. This allows you to develop a plan with specific coping strategies that you will know and be able to use when these factors seep into your lifestyle. Actually, some people are so accustomed to being constantly stressed, they literally have become addicted to stress and don't know how to act without it. This is the insidious nature of stress build up.

We all have stress. The only time we will be stress-free is when we're dead. We all have different stress limits. Reducing stress really is about how we handle and hold our stress. There is a story of a woman and a glass that has a lot to say about initially managing our stress. A woman explaining stress management to an audience, raised a glass of water and asked, "How heavy is this glass of water?" Answers ranged from 6 to 50 ounces. She replied, "The absolute weight doesn't matter. What matters is how long I hold it. If I hold it for a minute, that's not a problem. If I hold it for an hour, I'll have an ache in my right arm. If I hold it for a day, you might have to call an ambulance. In each case, it's the same weight, but the longer I hold it, the *heavier* it becomes." She continued by saying, "and that's the way it is with stress. If we carry all our burdens all of the time, sooner or later, as the burden becomes increasingly heavy, we won't be able to carry on. As it is with a glass of water; you must perceive the stressor, put it down for a while and rest before holding it again. When refreshed, we better cope with the burden giving one a new outlook and renewed energy."

So, it is critical to your overall *flight* or life plan that you know what causes you stress, begin to perceive it differently, learn to set it aside for a bit and address it when you have a better perception with a different attitude.

Allow me to help you identify and determine if you are under too much stress in your life making your *ride too bumpy or rough*. It is important to identify the physical effects of your stressors so that when you start feeling them, you can take action and do something constructive to prevent or deal with them as they arise.

Here is a list of physical signs that might tell you that you are under too much stress:

- Headaches or unexplained rashes on neck or face.
- Not sleeping well.
- Abnormally irritable.

- Sore muscles that were not strained.
- Constant fatigue.
- Withdrawal from activities previously enjoyed.
- Lack of motivation.
- Chest pains.
- Heavy, labored breathing, or often restless.

Simply put, the more of these signs you may have, the more stressed you may be. More stress means more damage to your health and your life. It is not a negative thing to identify that you have a lot of these indicators; however, it is an unhealthy choice to know them and do nothing about them! So, what can you effectively do to manage those stressors in your life? What can you do when your *flight* gets a bit bumpy?

Several important keys to managing your stress:

- Understanding that you need to be healthy and well in all eight dimensions of wellness: social, physical, emotional and mental, career, intellectual, environmental, spiritual and financial. If not, you need to identify which dimension(s) you are not well in. Then you need to begin to take the necessary wellness actions in that dimension.
- Balancing your life personally, professionally and with your family.
- Identifying your stressors before they cause you stress again.
- Identifying and tuning into those triggers that tell your mind or body that it is being affected by the stress.
- Practicing effective coping strategies that work for you including stress management and relaxation techniques.
- Practicing mindfulness techniques as well as mental imagery.

Stress management is about a conscious, well thought-out plan to take control and perceive your stressors differently. It also includes taking the necessary actions to reduce your stress as it rises. I would suggest you take some time to identify those people and events that bother or stress you. Make a list and then think about healthier ways you could handle those stressors.

Allow me to get very practical. After thirty years of teaching middle school adolescents and providing hundreds of stress management presentations to many employees from different organizations and businesses, below is a list of both relevant and practical coping strategies for those mental stressors that could definitely have a direct effect on your mind (thoughts) and your heart (feelings).

Relevant and practical coping strategies for your *mental* stressors:

- Set realistic goals for your day.
- Learn to intentionally plan your day with balance and for your priorities.
- Talk about your feelings with others - release them - liberate yourself emotionally.
- Don't be afraid to cry - endorphins are released.
- Take a deep breath and simply count to ten as you exhale.
- Practice positive chatter and self-talk.
- Exchange worry times with wishful or prayerful times.
- Become your own priority and intentionally plan to take care of yourself EVERY day.
- Refuse to let work dominate your life.
- Let go of your anger in healthy and positive ways.
- Distinguish between needs and wants.
- Keep an appreciation or gratitude journal.
- Write down your thoughts and feelings and throw them away.
- Again, learn to put things into perspective.
- Laugh... often and at yourself.
- Get your 12 touches needed daily.
- Learn to take mini vacations through mental imagery
- Practice mindfulness techniques.

- Seek professional help when you seem to have no control - by the way, this is a very healthy behavior.

Your mental stressors are different from your physical stressors and they need to be dealt with differently. As you make your list of things that bother or stress you, put an "M" or a "P" next to them to differentiate the two.

Relevant and practical coping strategies for your *physical* stressors:

- Sleep well. Figure out your best habits for a sound night's sleep so that sleep deprivation isn't one of your stressors.
- Eat well. Eating unbalanced meals can cause physical stress on many of your body's organs.
- Try to intentionally speak calmly when you are angry. Try it! You might like the control you have given yourself!
- When extremely busy, intentionally plan a relaxing date night out.
- Identify your physical triggers when stressed, so you can begin effective actions as they arise preventing a pile up of stress.
- Practice stress management: mental imagery and mindfulness techniques to deal with the physical stressors.
- Regularly schedule self-care: pedicures, manicures, massages, etc. to help with your physical stress.
- Begin to include intentional to 10 or 15 minutes of daily reflection time into your daily schedule. That could include time to sit, be calm, be thankful, pray, practice mindfulness and stress management techniques.
- Exercise more when you are physically stressed. Do things that are joyful and fun for you.
- Once you feel stress in your neck, back, arms, legs, shoulders, etc., focus on that muscle set and very slowly relax the set.

David Winograd has provided yet another thought-provoking poem regarding how some handle their stress in unhealthy ways.

A colleague once told me
He hated his job
His boss was a moron
His office mate a slob

He disliked the product
And the marketing pitch
He thought the spokesperson
Looked like a witch

He was constantly stressed
And snapped at everyone
It was painfully obvious
He was having no fun

So, I suggested this book
That I thought was great
I said it would help him
To set his life straight

It would take a commitment
For him to succeed
To provide him the tools
He would certainly need

But alas though I tried
To get into his head
He just drove to a bar
And got drunk instead

Well stated! Many people cope with their stressors in unhealthy ways. All that does is compound their problems and cause more stress. I strongly suggest choosing coping behaviors that are healthy and are beneficial to your overall health and future direction. Then you can *fly your plane* while NOT "under the influence" of unhealthy coping behaviors.

Sometimes things happen to cause large amounts of stress. *Your plane gets hi-jacked* in other words. Life isn't always smooth. Some stresses can change your life's direction such as your spouse, child or another family member dies, someone gets cancer, or a divorce occurs causing your life to become quite *turbulent*. Realize, this is part of life and part of the journey. Take care of yourself. Know that your flight might be *delayed or re-routed*, but the destination remains the same. Continue to focus on your vision as best you can while coping with the *turbulence*. Know that the horizon will get bright again. Life continually vacillates between highs and lows. If you continue to focus on your vision while coping with the immediate stressors, things will work themselves out in time and with faith.

Time to fly on my friends! Know that you really are in control. Keep in mind - MOST THINGS WILL WORK WELL AGAIN AND POSSIBLY MORE EFFICIENTLY IF YOU SIMPLY UNPLUG THEM FOR AWHILE! Remember, a diamond is a piece of charcoal that handled stress exceptionally well for thousands of years. So, put your positive, stress-reducing pants on and intentionally enjoy the *rest of your flight* in a more relaxed and intentional manner.

SAFE FLIGHT CHECKLIST:

- Stress is the root of many lifestyle diseases.
- Stress is universal and it most often boils down to how you perceive your stressors.
- There are many positive and healthy ways to cope with stress.
- YOU are the most important person when controlling your stress.

YOUR FLIGHT ACTION PLAN:

1. Choose one thing that stresses you. When that one stressor arises, exercise a new coping strategy that you have planned. Allow that coping strategy to become a habit. Then begin addressing another stressor. Challenge yourself and feel the confidence grow.
2. Starting immediately, practice catching yourself when you are feeling stressed. Ask yourself if this stress is being perceived as a stressor or if it is something you have no control over. If it is out of your control, let it go. Don't let it live in your head rent free.
3. Select one, two or three daily rituals that allow you to slow down, get off the roller coaster and just appreciate the moment. Be more peaceful and relaxed. Choose to relax and *enjoy your flight.*
4. Prepare for your *flight,* your life, with a written-out stress management plan that includes practical ways to deal with the never-ending stressors. Imagine it as your *carry-on bag* for your *flight for life.* You have access to that bag constantly, even when those simple physical stressors continue to arise like having to "go" in the airplane bathroom!

   - Go to the companion website at **www.intentionallivinguniversity.com** for more articles, suggested books, video clips, etc.

Chapter 12

Identifying your Purpose and Creating Your Life's Mission with Passion
"You are still in control as the pilot and you're almost to the runway"

As this book nears completion, as a matter of fact, so is your life despite whatever your age. As I have stated, time flies and before you know it, you will be looking back at your life, *your flight*, and recollecting your memories or loathing your regrets. This chapter will be an exciting one for you. It will also be a thought-provoking one. It will be an emotional chapter where you will be given the opportunity to acquire the necessary tools to write your own life's mission. This is your plan - your own vision to live the rest of your life. Imagine for a moment, you are piloting a plane and you have a personal responsibility to land it safely with confidence and ease. Think of those feelings you may have as you begin to descend and approach the runway. Nervous? Hopeful? Confident?

Begin to view the rest of your life as a long gradual and continual descent no matter your age. How do you want to feel?

What would you like to accomplish? How can you *land* the plane with few regrets? To begin truly living the rest of your *flight*, I challenge you to go back and identify your purpose and what is truly meaningful to you. Ask yourself, "Why am I flying this plane? What was my purpose in taking over the control panel in the cockpit and engaging the acceleration handle? What are the reasons I get up every day? What is my daily purpose for the rest of my life?" Think about those people, experiences, etc. that really mean something to you. Write them down. Own them. Like them. Feel confident about them. Believe in them. Begin to live according to them.

When you realize your "reason for being" and begin to focus on it daily, you will live with more intention, more passion and ON PURPOSE! It's critical to your *flight* for you to find your purpose and to plan daily on how you want to live for that purpose, by intention. Then, after some serious thought, write out and carefully design your life's PLAN, VISION, or what I call your *life's mission statement - LMS*! Researchers have concluded that it is only when people have meaning and purpose in their lives, do they experience healthy changes even at the cellular level. I challenge you to seriously think about it, write about it and intentionally integrate it into your daily plan including your attitude and perspective.

Your purpose may come from a very spiritual basis. It may not. Your purpose can be identified from thinking about your core values, your beliefs. Your purpose can be chosen, a new way of living, a new direction BY CHOICE! Your faith and environment will give you a multitude of ways to identify or realize your purpose. I strongly suggest you begin the process of writing your life's mission by deciding on your purpose first. If you already have one, great! If you are unsure, develop it, choose it and write it out.

We have all heard, "This is the first day of the rest of your life." Well, it really is. Believing this uplifting statement, allows you to liberate yourself from the mundane, unhappy life you may be presently living. It may seem overwhelming, maybe even a bit scary but it can also be extremely exciting. C.S. Lewis, an influential writer and an intellectual giant of the 20th century, wrote more than 30 books. He stated, "You can't go back and change the beginning, but you can start where you are and change the ending!" In this chapter, you will be given a special opportunity to carefully and thoughtfully PLAN how you would like to change your ending, your *descent* and truly and intentionally LIVE the rest of your LIFE! Arnold H. Glasow, a famous businessman from Wisconsin, wrote and sold a humor magazine to many businesses wrote his first book at the age of 92. He stated, "Make your life a mission-not an intermission." It is a profound statement and one that you may want to consider as a basis for your life's plan.

Right now, as you are reading this chapter, stop for a few moments and begin to think of what you really want for your future life. Don't just wish or dream. Honestly ask yourself, "What kind of life do I actually want for the rest of my life? What are the integral components of that desired life? How will I acquire those things I need to attain? How will I live with the necessary persistence and not stray from my written purpose and my plan?"

George Burns, the loved comedian, once stated, "Always look to the future since that'll be where you spend most of your time." Thinking about how you want to eventually live in your future can be rejuvenating itself! Most people spend more time planning their vacations and their weddings than they do their lives! Well, let us begin planning for your own life, your own *flight*, your own *descent* RIGHT NOW. I believe if you don't design your own life plan, you'll fall into someone else's. Chances are, they don't have a whole lot planned for you. Truly think about these two statements and allow them to motivate you to begin the process of writing your own vision, your own attainable plan.

A line from Lewis Carroll's book, *Alice's Adventures in Wonderland* says, "If you don't know where you are going, any road will get you there."13 This line characterizes many unhappy and unsuccessful people in life. They don't think of living for a PURPOSE and on PURPOSE. They just habitually or routinely think about going to work, paying the bills and raising their families. In contrast, happy and successful people find a way to live a life of happiness, meaning and purpose. They also live a more balanced life personally, professionally and familywise, by choice and by daily intention. Your life, without a purpose or plan allows your achievements to seem hollow, your future to be uncertain and your present conditions to be chaotic.

Try not to get distracted by the views of others. Focus on what engages and inspires you. The most exhilarating experiences in your life will be those generated in your mind and then triggered by information that challenges your thinking, like the content in this book. If you are passionate about something and those around you are not, all that should matter to you is that YOU ARE - period! Progressive and revolutionary thinkers who take action and begin change are driven by their identified passions, not whether or not others around them are passionate or motivated.

Before I begin explaining the process, I would like to remind you of a quote by Helen Keller, "The most pathetic person in the world is a person that has sight but no vision." So, it goes for us. We all need a vision, a plan, a *flight pattern* to guide us daily, allow us to *pilot* successfully and remind us how we really want to live the rest of our lives.

Allow me to begin this invigorating and exciting process. First, value the experience of thinking about, developing and writing your desired plan FOR YOUR LIFE! This is huge. Many people are not given this opportunity. Let me define what a life's mission entails. It is a written statement and used as a reminder to live a life of purpose with an intentional healthy balance between your career, your personal life and your family life. It is a vision on how you want to live a healthier life inclusive of the eight dimensions of wellness. The statement should include a desired life, planned with a personally chosen attitude each day and one that will be lived with true passion. The plan intentionally focuses on hope and anticipation with your personal goals and items on your bucket list so you can live your life with few regrets. As you begin to think about it and write it, you won't construct it, you'll detect it. It's already there based on your inner core values, principles and beliefs.

I would like to share a few reminders and specific techniques that allows you the opportunity to successfully and more naturally write your mission statement.

My reminders include:

- Feel free to use acronyms, song titles, words, quotes, sayings, etc. as a basis for the construction of your LMS.
- Brevity is a virtue. You probably won't read a dissertation daily. Keep your mission statement between 100-400 words. Use your creativity.
- Try a variety of the strategies or techniques suggested and use the one that works best for you.
- Go to YouTube and access and view desired clips of other people and their thoughts and processes of writing a life's mission statement.
- Make sure your LMS includes your purpose, the eight dimensions of your overall wellness, intended balance between your personal, professional and family lives as well as your items on your bucket list.

When you think you are completed, ask yourself the following questions:

- Have I stated my purpose to live, my reason(s) to get up every day and truly engage in that day?
- Does my LMS put my problems that may arise into perspective?

- Does my LMS provide me with the positive attitude I want for each day, complete with a plan for happiness and success?
- Does my LMS address my specific goals or items on my bucket list so, if attained, I can have lived a life with few regrets?
- Does my LMS intentionally allow me to better balance my life personally, professionally and with my family?
- Does my LMS provide me with a specific and desired plan to intentionally live each day with passion?
- Does my LMS allow me to incorporate "me-time" to care for myself personally, so I can effectively care for others when necessary.

If you can answer yes to each one of the questions above, you've written your initial *living flight plan* - your life's mission statement.

There are many techniques to writing your mission statement. Several sites on the internet will provide you with some assistance in writing your mission statement. I would like to personally suggest two techniques that have worked for many of the teens and adults that I have helped facilitate in developing their mission statements. You can find the working documents on the companion website for this chapter.

TECHNIQUE # 1:

Technique number one includes simply answering all the questions below and then pulling your answers together in a culminating mission statement.

Questions to ask yourself as you prepare to write your life's mission statement:

- What has been your purpose in life so far? What would you like it to be?
- What have you given or provided to others thus far in your life?

- What are your core beliefs about life?
- What has given you the greatest sense of meaning and purpose in your life?
- What has brought you joy, happiness, peace and contentment to this point in your life?
- What has brought you success?
- What has been one of the most important crossroads in your life thus far?
- How have you taken care of yourself in each of the eight dimensions of wellness?
- Have you regretted doing or not doing something?
- What has been the best advice someone gave you about living?
- What do you wish you would have learned sooner?
- Are you living a balanced life personally, professionally and with your family?
- Have you consciously thought about and written out your bucket list? How about your spousal bucket list? How about your family bucket list?
- Have you written out the goals you have for the rest of your life?
- Have you written out a personally designed plan for how you would like to live your life from now on moving forward?
- Has spirituality played a significant role in your life?
- What is your greatest fear at the end of your life?
- Now that you are older, what are your views of living? Your views of death?
- What do you think matters most for you to find true happiness?
- What would you like to pay a lot less attention to in your life?
- If you had to give yourself some valuable advice on how to enjoy your life, what might it be?
- What kind of attitude would you like to have daily?
- What legacy might you like to leave behind for others?
- What changes could you make to better your life?

- What changes do you <u>need</u> to make to better your life?
- What are those things you can do to make a genuine difference in the lives of those you love and to those around you?

TECHNIQUE # 2:

The second technique is titled, "My Retirement Banquet." First, think for a moment that you are at your own retirement banquet. You are 65 years young.

A. Briefly list a few adjectives that you would want the following people to say about you.

Husband/Wife/Significant other

Colleagues

Children

Parent(s)

Family

Friends

***What you have listed are a few adjectives, traits and characteristics you think are necessary and important to your style of living. Remember these when you begin to write the purpose portion of your life's mission statement.

B. Next, are three areas of your life. Identify what changes you wish you would have made during your years of employment that could have balanced your overall life better.

Personally

Professionally

With your Family

***What you have listed here are the possible things you wanted to change but never did for whatever reason. Realize these things can still be changed and incorporated into your life's mission - your vision - your plan for the rest of your life - that last chapter!

C. Identify any changes you would have liked to have made in the following 8 dimensions of your wellness during those years of employment.

Social

Physical

Emotional/Mental

Career

Intellectual

Environmental

Spiritual

Financial

***What you have written here are the behavioral changes that you still may want to make in order to live a happy, lengthy life with few regrets.

D. Think about and list of some of your desired life goals or items on a "bucket list" that were not achieved during your years of employment:

***What is listed here are those goals and bucket list items you never had time for while working! Now you do! Remember, happy and successful people "spend" their time on their priorities and manage their time wisely, based on their priorities.

E. Think of a quote, song title, bit of wisdom or an acronym that might describe your employment years. Imagine it being shared as a huge banner at your retirement party. Now, imagine another banner that will describe your future plan for the years you have remaining in your life.

*** What you have written are core beliefs that have described your life thus far and your new vision for your future. Think about what you have written when writing your new life's mission statement - you might see the need to combine the two sets of beliefs.

F. Finally, imagine someone has asked you, while at your banquet, to verbally share your future retirement plan, your mission, your vision, your overall plan to live the rest of your life. Using what you have thought about and learned in the previous chapters in this book, write a brief and concise statement that would include:

- Your purpose and choice of daily attitude
- Your thoughts on your priorities and how you spend time.
- Your thoughts on life balance.
- Your thoughts on living well within the eight dimensions of wellness.
- Your bucket list items.

Saying this statement verbally before you write it will help you conserve on words and paraphrase where needed.

*** What you have written is the foundation of your life's mission. Yippee! Yahoo! Feel proud! Your statement will most likely require some tweaking and should remain as a living-working document as your life changes.

Just a reminder, this book is primarily about YOU taking control of the remaining years of your life. Understand this may include your spiritual core values, a higher power, faith and God. He or that higher power can be the *pilot* and you the *co-pilot* if you so desire. That spirit, higher power or God can be guiding you. However, you ultimately have the free will to make the choices you want regarding your life on this earth. Remember, your higher power, faith or God can be communicating to you with support from their *Control Tower* and positively act as your *co-pilot*.

When you think you are finally done, ask yourself the following questions to assure that your life's mission statement is complete:

- Does it give me a relevant and practical plan to live daily with intention and with purpose?
- Does it remind me to live a balanced life?
- Does it remind me of my choice of the attitude I want for each day?
- Does it address my priorities in life and how I intend to "spend" my time?
- Does it provide the necessary reminder to help me with the ability to put things into perspective and address those challenges that come up daily?
- Will it allow me to love more deeply and simply appreciate the moments more often?
- Does it provide hope and anticipation so that when I pass away, I'll die without any major regrets?

Once completed, the most important piece has yet to occur - the implementation portion of the process. That is, deciding how you will take specific action and LIVE your life's mission statement. Will you share it with loved ones? Will you post it in a frame and display it in several places to act as a constant reminder of how you are choosing to live differently? Will you save it as a screensaver on your phone, iPad or laptop? Will you sign it as a contract to yourself? Will you put a copy of it in your wallet or purse? How about a copy on your bathroom mirror where you prepare yourself for the day? How about a copy on the passenger side sun visor in your car? What about hanging it on a keychain? How about all of these?

I have made several inferences to your life and you being the *pilot*. The story you are about to read encapsulates the overall thought process of writing and then living the rest of your life's mission.

Two men sat next to each other on an airplane. One was a pilot, en route to catch his next flight, a large 767. The non-pilot asked him about his instrument landings. The pilot replied, "Oh, the new planes have the capability of landing in what they call zero-zero." That means while in the air, the pilot can see zero feet in front of the plane. When the pilot lands, visibility remains zero. The second man responded that to land in total blindness like that, you really have to trust your instruments. The pilot replied that an aircraft has three computers on board, each is checking to make sure that everything is correct. If just one of the computers disagrees with the other two, they abort the landing, circle and try it again. All three computers, checking the same data, must agree that everything is in order to bring the plane safely to the ground. Your life can be similar to that process of landing. Know that it may have to take you through some clouds, some possible darkness and maybe even some rough times. Your life's mission plan will automatically allow your head which is your mind, your heart which includes your feelings and your life – which represents the three computers on-board which are your safety checks.

As you age, you will have to double-check and triple-check your *flight path* home. This will allow for your descent to be both a smooth and safe one with few regrets. Maybe choose a co-pilot, your spouse, significant other or a friend to assist with your navigation. Disengage your *autopilot*, doing the same unintentional and mundane things day after day, and *fly* your own plane living your own predestined life.

Pilots use another term called RVR or Runway Visibility Reading. We need to have a vision for our *runway* - for our eventual descent. Your RVR will come to life when you write your life's mission statement.

When completed to your satisfaction, you will have written your very own *flight manual.* I am so excited for you! As you implement this personally designed plan into your life, realize once again, you ARE the pilot of the only life you will ever be given. You are flying the plane; you are in control and you may be in the descent phase of your flight.

Fly well, my friend, with intention and purpose while living differently by choice and by design. Don't give up! Live with purpose. Someday, you may be that nurse or doctor that saves a life, that teacher that transforms lives daily or that politician that makes policy for impactful positive change. You might be the one with a gentle touch to hold the hand of a dying spouse or a special friend. Do not give up! Live with passion and purpose while on your mission. You have no idea how much the world needs you or how important your purpose will become.

SAFE FLIGHT CHECKLIST:

- A written out and regularly read mission statement will allow you to live with more intention, a more directed purpose and hopefully with more passion.
- If you don't have a plan on how you want to live the rest of your life, others in your life will definitely shape one FOR YOU.
- A vision, a mission or a plan for your life will provide more opportunities for wellness, balance and goal attainment.
- Your mission will allow you to live a life based on your values and priorities so you can get to your *destination* with few regrets.

YOUR FLIGHT ACTION PLAN:

1. Pick a quiet reflective time within the next 48-96 hours. In your daily planner, begin to write your vision, your plan or your life's mission statement with any desired techniques shared. Begin to *navigate* the rest of the LIFE you have planned for!
2. Enjoy the thinking, reflecting, planning and writing process. Appreciate the opportunity. Take your time. Think, write, rewrite, think, feel, write, rewrite.
3. Consider joint mission plan with your spouse or significant other life's mission plan and then plan the necessary time to write it and LIVE it!
4. Consider a family life's mission plan and then plan the necessary time to write it and LIVE it.
5. LIVE more contently, more satisfied, more happily - live differently!

ENJOY YOUR FLIGHT!

- Go to the companion website at **www.intentionallivinguniversity.com** for more articles, suggested books, video clips, etc.

Chapter 13

Creating an Epidemic with Others
"Getting others to fly with YOU - Creating a ripple effect"

    The final chapter? **NO!** Look at it as the **FIRST** chapter in **YOUR** newly designed life. Your creative, life-altering architectural plan inclusive of your passions, your intentional ways of living, your priorities and your chosen strategies to balance your life.

    Now that you have either begun the process of writing your life's mission statement or have completed *the flight plan process* and are *flying*, you can intentionally plan to be positively "infectious" with your new thinking, feelings and way of living. This new feeling you may be experiencing could be compared to the emotions you might have after completing your very first flight as a pilot. Think about what you are feeling: confident, happy, proud and successful. You can now begin to create an epidemic with those around you and create a massive ripple-effect. How do you get your spouse or significant other, your friends or your colleagues to *join you on your flight?* The answer is quite simple. JUST LIVE your plan. Live it happily with intention, passion, direction and that visible positive attitude. Be the person they want to emulate. That's all! Live to enjoy your life while "positively infecting" others creating an *epidemic* with those in your life.

Just the thought of your ability to positively influence others by a shining example and possibly change their lives is an extremely satisfying one. Your challenge: Get others to *FLY* and learn how to become the *pilot* of their own lives! Allowing others to see the magnificent changes in your life, may encourage them to learn your *piloting skills.*

In other words, invite others to be on your *flight team* so they can fly with you. The worst they could say is no. If you don't ask them, they won't get onboard. Believe me, you will want to share your newly designed plan and your new vision for your life with your team. Each one, as they *come aboard* are added to *your flight manifest* adding more energy to you and your *flight team.* The goal is to have a *stand-by* waiting list of people that really want to get on your plane. Live your life with the renewed energy and vision chosen by design. Don't waste your energy on those who don't want to fly with you. Don't take it personally. Worrying about people who really aren't ready to change will simply zap your energy.

How do you get others to understand what you are embracing? Maybe make your own website and invite those you care about or love to that site. For example, www.newvision4mylife.com was created to help people improve lives while affecting others. Get those people you care about and love to learn how you came to your vision, how you are living it, how you are feeling and have them buy into it on their own accord. THEY must want to change and plan just like you have done! You may begin to feel a nervous excitement for your life since it may be uncharted territory - a different way of living.

Allowing creativity to enter your lifestyle will sustain your renewed energy, plan or vision. Realize there will be setbacks, like bumps during a flight. Life is full of setbacks. Try and put each *bump* into perspective, learn from it and grow as a person. Learn to return to your *flight pattern - your life's course* and *fly* smoothly once again. Your energy for your vision and your plan must be greater than any life setback or anyone's negativity. Your belief in yourself and your plan has to be greater than those who may doubt you and sabotage your vision by intentionally depleting your energy.

Jim Valvano, one of the greatest college basketball coaches of all time, has a quote that should make us think. He stated, "To me, there are three things we all need to do every day of our lives. Number one is to laugh. We should all strive to find humor and laughter in our lives each and every day. Number two is to think. Spend more time in thought. And number three is, you should have your emotions moved to tears from happiness or joy. Think about it. If you laugh, think, and cry all in a day, that's a good day. That's a heck of a day. You do that seven days a week, you're in for something special."[14]

Continue your vision while living your plan until it is an embedded way of life. It becomes a habit. Trust and believe that good things will happen every day you wake. Keep an open eye for them as somedays they may be very insignificant. Realize you could *crash* at any time, BUT having the faith, the vision and your habitual plan, doesn't allow for the excessive worry for major catastrophes. Don't be afraid to use your *oxygen masks* or things that motivate you and provide you passion. Let that refresh you and take control of any strong emotion that may try to steer your life in a different direction. Begin to live more freely, not by the *panel controls*, but by your heart. Be enthusiastic about your life every day. After all, you can't light a fire with a wet match. Make your enthusiasm contagious! Choose to be exciting every single morning. Starting your day like this, attracts more future *passengers* and helps them energize as they *fly their flight*. As the *pilot* of your life, love your *passengers*, those people in your life that care for and love you: spouses, children, family members, friends and possibly even colleagues.
Be a positive force. Influence those you love and your co-workers by:

- Thinking before you speak.
- Keeping an open mind.
- Choosing to debate vs. argue.
- Speaking with a soft, calm voice no matter what.
- Missing no opportunity for praising someone or giving them a kind word.
- Listening to and assimilating your loved one's expectations.
- Learning to take personal constructive criticism.
- Respecting the feelings of others.
- Becoming more emotionally intelligent.
- Refusing to discuss the weaknesses of others.
- Letting your virtues, your vision and your life plan speak for itself.

According to Jon Gordon in his book, *The Energy Bus*, he states that there are five ways to *love your passenger*s:15

- Make time for them.
- Listen to them.
- Recognize them.
- Serve them.
- Bring out the best in them.

What a great bus ride or *flight* this would be for all involved. *Pilot* your *flight* with these five items in mind. Your *passengers* will love you and you will be a living legacy.

You may never know who needs you. Positive energy is absolutely contagious. Go ahead and be intentionally infectious in a positive way each and every day you live. So, it is my heart-felt wish that you *fly* with a renewed purpose and a new vision. You now have the ultimate *jet-fuel,* the knowledge and strategies from this book. It is your time to *fly*, really live and *enjoy the flight*.

While being "infectious" and creating your epidemic, realize this adapted quote from an unknown author. "If you seek to live in accordance with your spirit, higher power or God's will for your life, you will live in accordance with certain 'commandments' or rules of living. You could study their words and be watchful for their signs. They often use you in wonderful and unexpected ways if you use those signs." Stay confident and true to yourself and use your faith, strong values and beliefs to help direct your intentional plan to LIVE! While living your plan, make sure you have incorporated *contingency flight plans* such as life vests, parachutes, oxygen masks, as these are available and required on all aircrafts. What will you use as a *backup plan* to live your life's mission?

You now have the ultimate *jet-fuel*, the knowledge and strategies from this book. It is your time to *fly*, really live and *enjoy the flight*.

David Winograd shares one last poem that I believe sums up my entire book.

As this book was written
I was given the chapters
To peruse and proofread
I discovered what matters

To live a full life
You must plan and prepare
If you let it just happen
You will never get there

What's important to you
Are the things you must find
And the actions to take
Of both body and mind

Take hold of the happy
Get rid of the gloom
You will look and feel better
You'll light up the room

So, with purpose and passion
And much introspection
You'll just be amazed
At your new life's direction!

It could not be stated any clearer! Begin the ripple effect and positively live your life to the fullest, while "infecting" others in a positive way!

SAFE FLIGHT CHECKLIST:

- Intentionally "infecting" others with your new lifestyle can be very beneficial to many.
- Don't waste your energy on those who *don't want to fly with you.*
- Good energy is contagious.
- Your vision, plan or mission will become reality if it is important enough.

YOUR FLIGHT ACTION PLAN:

1. Identify those people in your life who you think could help you *fly the plane* or *be the co-pilot.* Share your plan, your new vision and ask for their help, understanding and support.

2. Incorporate your vision and purpose using some or all of the flight action plan suggestions at the end of each chapter to write the beginning foundation of your life's mission, your plan and your vision.

3. Begin NOW to choose to live the life that YOU want. Don't wait for chance or destiny to make your life simply occur. You are motivated.

4. When done with this **life masterpiece**, make copies, display and share with your *passengers*!

Let's Get After It!

- Go to the companion website at **www.intentionallivinguniversity.com** for more articles, suggested books, video clips, etc.

MY CONCLUSION.....YOUR BEGINNING!

My hope is that I've provided you with many thoughts to consider, along with relevant and life changing information. This information will provide an extremely valuable opportunity to literally write yourself a new way of living the rest of your life.

It was my devoted intention to help you create a vision of your design to live your life differently; in a way you might not have considered living your life before.

You've most likely read many books prior to this one. The process of reading my book was hopefully an experience, one you will not only take action on, but also share with those important to you in your life.

I'd like to conclude with one last metaphor. I would like to give you a gift. A *free flight,* one where YOU are the pilot and in total control, one that will differ from any other flight you will EVER take again. Take the *e-ticket* in your hand and consider it an invitation - an important invitation.

I strongly encourage you to take that first step onto the *walkway* down into your plane!

Before you take this *flight,* in which you will *pilot*, make sure you take the necessary time to write your life's mission plan, your vision. Go ahead and with confidence and pride sit down in the cockpit. After getting situated and familiar with all the instruments and controls, prepare YOURSELF for a smooth take-off and begin living your life as YOU have planned. Hopefully, your *flight* will be a lengthy one without having to stray from your *flight pattern*, one with loads of happiness and an abundance of joy. As you come to a *safe landing at your destination* with few regrets, you'll be able to look back and say, **"What a ride, what a flight!"**

NOW BOARDING!

The BEGINNING of the rest of your flight is waiting for YOU!

This poem titled, *Invictus,* by William Ernest Henley recaps this entire book.

Invictus

Out of the night that covers me,
Black as the pit from pole to pole,
I thank whatever gods may be
For my unconquerable soul

In the fell clutch of circumstance
I have not winced or cried aloud.
Under the bludgeonings of chance
My head is bloody but unbowed

Beyond this place of wrath and tears
Looms the Horror of the shade,
And yet the menace of the years
Finds and shall find me unafraid.

It matters not how strait the gate,
How charged with punishments the scroll,
I am the master of my fate,
I am the captain of my soul.

"The only person you are destined to become is the person you decide to be"

Ralph Waldo Emerson

The BEGINNING of the rest of your flight is waiting for YOU

References

1. Covey, Stephen R., *The 7 Habits of Highly Effective People*. Simon and Schuster, 1989.

2. Buettner, Dan, *The Blue Zones Solution: Eating and Living Like the World's Healthiest People*. National Geographic Society, 2015.

3. Rohn, Jon, www.myowneulogy.com.

4. Prochaska and DiClemente, 1983, Prochaska and Norcross, 1992, Transtheoretical Model of Change.

5. U.S. Department of Health and Human Services, Surgeon General Report 1990.

6. Maraboli, Steve, stevemaraboli.net.

7. Ellis, Linda, "The Dash,"www.lindaellis.com.

8. Buettner, Dan, *Thrive: Finding Happiness the Blue Zone Way*. National Geographic Society, 2010.

9. Lombardo, Elizabeth. *A Happy You: Your Ultimate Prescription for Happiness*. Seal Press, 2014.

10. Aubele, Teresa, *Train Your Brain to Get Happy*. Adams Media, 2011.

11. Nakia Gordon Ph.D., Psychology, Bowling Green State University.

12. Shimoff, Marci, with Carol Kline. *Happy for No Reason: 7 Steps to Being Happy from the inside Out*. Free Press 2009.

13. Carroll, Lewis, *Alice's Adventures in Wonderland*, Macmillan, November 1865.

14. Jim Valvano, North Carolina State University Head Basketball Coach, 1980-1990.

15. Gordon, Jon, *The Energy Bus: 10 Rules to Fuel Your Life, Work, and Team with Positive Energy*. John Wiley and Sons, Inc., 2007.

53649319R00085

Made in the
USA
Lexington, KY